My
America

My America

Dennis Luksza

authorHOUSE®

AuthorHouse™
1663 Liberty Drive
Bloomington, IN 47403
www.authorhouse.com
Phone: 1-800-839-8640

First published by AuthorHouse   11/29/2011

ISBN: 978-1-4670-7669-2 (sc)
ISBN: 978-1-4670-7668-5 (hc)
ISBN: 978-1-4670-7667-8 (ebk)

Library of Congress Control Number: 2011919246

Printed in the United States of America

Intro

Before reading this book I feel obligated to inform you that my detractors will state that my solutions are too simplistic. That my solutions couldn't possibly work. But I fully believe that my solutions to our problems should be simple. The solutions should be easily understood. This book will be extremely short because I am not a professional writer as you will be able to tell immediately. As my old English teacher used to say when someone asked how long a paper or essay had to be "Make it as long as a girl skirt". When the perplexed student asked what he meant, the teacher would reply that the paper needed to be long enough to cover the subject but short enough to be interesting. (If I could remember this teacher's name I would mention it, but I cannot.) I have done my best to take his advice. I think quality is much more important than quantity.

I have spent countless hours thinking about our problems in America. I have played the what if game. What if we did this or that and then realized for one reason or another it was a stupid idea. However, once good ideas started coming they came very fast. So, now let's get into what this book is about.

This book is about my solutions to the most important problems America is now facing. I will offer workable solutions. I will present a plan that explains how we could fix these problems. I will explain why I feel these solutions have not been offered before. (At least I don't think they have been offered before.) I will explain the obstacles that we would have in instigating these solutions.

The problems that I am referring to are: 1) unemployment, 2) affordable health care for all, 3) our national debt, 4) our dependence on foreign oil, 5) pollution in our environment, 6) social security, 7) single parent family units, 8) retirement, 9) our politicians, 10) an unfair burden on the middle class. In addressing these problems I will show how the following things can be implemented: 1) full employment, 2) health care for everyone, 3) our national debt being repaid at an rapid rate, 4) no dependence on foreign oil, 5) a healthier environment, 6) a better nation, 7) earlier full retirement, 8) a social security system that has a surplus (year to year) such that we need to figure how much in raises social security recipients should get each year, 9) an equitable way to pay our health care insurance and social security, 10) family units becoming more and more the norm, 11) employers and employees working together with more and more benefits for both, 12) retirees young enough to enjoy their golden years, 13) a shrinking poor population, 14) a better life for most Americans, and 15) congressmen and women doing their jobs. By incorporating all these ideas and many more all the items I just listed could and should be accomplished.

My purpose in writing this book is to get enough attention from the public to get some of these things done. I hope I have peaked your interest. I will tackle more than one problem jointly. I will begin with full employment, early retirement and social security.

Chapter 1

Full employment, fixing social security and early retirement are the most pressing issues we face today. They are also the simplest to fix.

In order to see where I am coming from you have to make 3 assumptions: 1) We have enough jobs (we have too many workers) 2) The government should not be spending money to create phony jobs. 3) Everyone needs to pay their fair share.

My fix would be in overhauling social security and if need be adding a 1% sales tax. Let's look at part of social security. Remember, social security started out as a social insurance not a retirement plan. When our stock market collapsed and our banks went belly up many retirement plans went broke. Citizens who were playing the stock market lost their retirement funds. Social security became their only means of retirement. Now seniors are waiting for full social security retirement. What is full retirement with social security? Full retirement refers to the age at person can retire, draw social security with full benefits. So what age is that? Well, that depends on when you were born. In 1956 widows of covered workers could retire with full benefits at age 62. Now, depending on when you were born, full social security starts at age 65, 66, or 67. (Kind of like the shell game. When you get close they move the pieces around.)

If you were born prior to 1938 your full retirement under social security would be at age 65. If you were born in 1938 or after, your full social security age would increase by 2 months each ensuing year until 1943 where your full social security retirement is achieved at age 66 and where it stays until the birth year of 1955 when the full retirement social security age begins increasing again every 2 months ending their increase in the 1960 year of birth where full social security benefits are received at age 67. The reason this is done is to keep social security solvent. I believe we are completely backward in our thinking. By the time our young people reach age 67 full social security retirement might be 120. Then social security would be solvent forever. (Goal achieved!)

Realistically, many Americans 62 and older would retire if they could. Let's help them. Think about the ramifications if the baby boomers started retiring earlier than anticipated. What would happen to unemployment? As I see it, earlier and earlier retirement should be a goal of government. It should not be feared. We have this notion about retirement completely backward. So how do we get to this full employment, earlier retirement, and solvent social security? We must be willing to do four things. 1) Remove the $106,800 cap. People who earn more than that quit paying social security tax. If you earn a million dollars a year you would pay social security tax on the full million. 2) You cap the amount any one person can receive in a one year period. Say $100,000 a year (this would not affect many people or their lifestyles, but would add a huge base to social security) 3) Lower full retirement age to 62 or 63 (forget the shell game). 4) If necessary enact a 1% sales tax, no exceptions. This revenue would go directly into a trust fund for social security. If these changes were made, social security would have a surplus of funds forever. You would have huge numbers of people retiring. This would create more jobs than could be filled.

I believe these changes would work and be fair. I also believe we should be striving for early retirement. Like it or not social security has become a retirement fund. With the overhauling of social security it would become more fair. Why should a millionaire not pay social security on earnings over $106,800?

I am from St. Louis, therefore, a huge Cardinal baseball fan so I am going to use the Cardinals as an example. If one of the Cardinals makes 17 million dollars a year, do you think he will change his lifestyle if he has to pay social security on the whole $17 million? Do you think he will need to draw more than $100,000 a year from social security when he retires? The answer to me is obviously no.

Social security started out at 4%. Your employer paid 2% and you paid 2%. It is now 13.3%. Your employer pays 7.65% and you pay 5.65% up until we get to the $106,800 cap. Just for fun let's use the Cardinal player who makes $17 million a year as an example. He pays 5.65% on that $106,800 which comes to $6,034. What percent is that of earnings of $17 million? How about 0.00035494. How much would 5.65% of $17 million be? $960,500. The employer pays 7.65%. 7.65% of 106,800 is $8170. What percent is $8170 of $17 million? The answer is 0.0004805. If the employer paid 7.65% on the entire $17 million he would pay $1,300,500. If the employer and employee each paid their fair share they would have paid $2,261,000 instead of the $15,204 they pay under the current system.

A $2,245,796 gain is hardly worth mentioning. There aren't many $17 million a year people. But there are a lot of people who make $106,800 or more, including our congressmen who make at least $175,000 a year. If the middle class and the poor pay 5.65% on social security, why is it fair that the wealthy pay a substantially smaller percentage? They certainly could afford to pay more. If the employer pays 7.65% on all their employees, why can't that employer pay 7.65%

on their most expensive employees? The answer, of course, goes back to our lawmakers.

The two provisions that I talked about before getting sidetracked were removing the cap on the amount you pay into social security and adding a cap to what you can collect annually. These two provisions are very fair and equitable. The early retirement is crucial in making America better. Let the elderly retire while they are still young enough to be active, young enough to spend money. I feel if the sales tax is deemed necessary to keep social security with a surplus forever and make earlier and earlier retirement possible, then it's a small price to pay. If the tax isn't needed, wonderful!

In my America citizens would be retiring and drawing social security earlier and earlier. For example, why not retire at age 50-55? I feel the sales tax is the most equitable way of financing something. The rich buy more. The middle class and poor buy what they can afford. So everyone pays their fair share.

Some other reasons I feel that a sales tax is the most fair way to pay for our needs: 1) you are spending within your means, 2) unlike personal property tax where the rich have found ways to avoid paying their share, a fair sales tax is something they would have a very hard time avoiding. An example of why a property tax is unfair is the fact that not all states have a property tax. The wealthy in states that have property tax simply register their yachts or cars in states that do not have property tax. 3) A sales tax is easily collected.

I know a lottery is another idea, but I feel that any time you encourage gambling that is a bad idea. The revenue generated would be the gamblers and not shared. I feel that if we are to fix America, then all Americans must join forces. With a sales tax you would include all Americans.

If the President insists on borrowing money for a stimulus package, then just dump it into social security. However, I believe that borrowing money and adding to a debt for any reason is a bad idea.

When reading and listening to our politician's different job plans, I feel they are missing the boat. I see the problem as us having too many workers and not enough consumers to grow our economy. Tax breaks are just good for corporations. If there is more consumers demanding their products, jobs will increase period, regardless of the tax breaks.

By implementing the 2 caps and the sales tax we would have early retirement and add new and unemployed workers to our work force. We would have a new group of seniors who would be spending money. If you take all this into account you would stimulate the economy and make Americans the envy of all other nations. You would reduce the number of poor Americans and jobs would be plentiful.

To me these changes are easy and they make sense. So why are they not done or even considered? Because for these changes to take place, Congressmen and women would have to rework social security in such a way that would not benefit the Congressmen and women. They would have to go against the two forces that, I believe, drive current-day politicians. Those two forces are or mandates are: 1) does this change make more money for me, and 2) does this change help my reelection campaign. When the answers to those questions is: no I will not make more money and no this will not help my reelection campaign, there is no chance for implementation. In fact, these changes would cost the congressmen and women money. Remember, their base salary is $175,000 so they would have to pay more social security taxes. Also, their rich supporters would have to pay more social security taxes. Their rich supporters would not be happy about this and contributions to their election campaigns might dwindle. So really, there is nothing to gain and everything to lose as far as the politicians are concerned.

I know they talk about full employment, but most of their ideas center on new jobs that they can use federal dollars to create these jobs. They are able to do favors and collect favors to and from lobbyists and this type of employment/jobs is phony. The work lasts for a specific time. The employer is given grants to pay for the labor and actually get the work done for virtually nothing (maybe a favor here or there). These types of jobs do not help our economy. They, in fact, add to our debt. They do, however, accomplish two things. The make the congressman or women more money or favors and they do help with the election campaign. The lobbyists or manufacturers who received the cheap labor are delighted. The politician can point to his bill that reduced unemployment. So you see why this unemployment problem is so big.

To actually solve the unemployment problem as I suggested would hurt the politicians. No longer would they be able to create these phony jobs. The jobs that we have might increase when a larger number of young retirees begin spending their money. In any event, we would shrink the workforce so the need for workers would be very high. Benefits would increase as well as pay. More families would be working and, I like to think, this would be one thing that would help the family unit stay together. The way things are now, I believe, there is not incentive for our congressmen and women to really solve the unemployment problem. The only reason they bother to talk about it is the effect it could have on their reelection. As long as they can fool the public with their phony, costly jobs, that are usually temporary, they have no fear of their reelection being affected.

My plan is simple, straightforward, fair and it would work. We would have full employment, a secure social security and early retirement if it were to be implemented. As America is now this can never be. I believe lawmakers can see this but the plain and simple truth is that lawmakers are accountable to their reelection campaign, their lobbyists and the wealthiest Americans. I also believe that they are driven by greed and unless bills have to do with making it better for them, they are not interested.

In my America politicians would be working for the masses. They would want a younger base of retirees spending money. They would like to see real full time employment. They would be willing to pay their fair share. They would base what to do on whether it is good or bad for America as a whole. They would not base what to do on whether it made them more money or was good for their reelection campaign.

Another thought on jobs is that the lobbyists fighting for a wealthy corporations is worried about how many more millions of dollars they can make. They don't care about jobs. Their concern is money. So if they need more workers to sell their products they will employ more workers. Plain and simple. A tax break is nice and helps the corporation make more money but does not lead to more jobs. Unless there is more demand for a product the work force will level out. However, if you increase the demand by having a larger base of consumers you will increase the demand for goods and services. Therefore, full retirement at an early age plus full employment equals more jobs. I believe this is a simple logical conclusion.

In closing this chapter, let me just say the first three changes are absolutely necessary. The two caps taking and paying, plus the early retirement are mandatory. The fourth part, the 1% sales tax, I'm not sure if that would be needed. I don't have enough fingers and toes to count the total money we would need to pull off my proposal. But I believe a mathematician with a computer and a calculator is just waiting. I feel that with the sales tax we would have a huge base. Without the sales tax it would be harder. In any event, in my America full employment with real jobs is easily obtained. Our social security system is not only sustainable, but would have a huge surplus forever. Our seniors could retire early, spend money and enjoy the end of their lives. Here is a sample of my bill on dealing with social security and unemployment:

Social security adjustment bill 3711 is as follows:

I   Lifting the income ceiling on social security
II   Applying a cap on social security money that can be paid out in a one year period
III A sales tax for social security
IV   Who will administer this bill

Section I

1) The 106,800 dollar income cap, where you stop paying social security will be removed with no ceiling cap in it's place. For example if you earn 17 million dollars a year you will pay social security on 17 million dollars a year as will your employer. And the percentage you pay on social security will remain the same no matter the dollar amount you earn. The money generated from removing this cap will be put into purchasing treasury bonds and put into a special social security account.

Section II

1) There will be a cap of 100,000 dollars that can be paid out to any one retiree in a one year period.

Section III

1) There will be a 1% national sales tax on all items purchased in the United States (including on line purchases). The money from this sales tax will go into purchasing treasury bonds. And added to a special social security account. This will be the same account that all social security revenue is in. The social security account will not be placed in or used for anything other than funds for retirement. The revenue from this social security account is forbidden from being placed into general revenue and used for anything than it's intended purposes. The intended purposes for the money in the social security account are: 1) Lower full early retirement age 2) Give raises to retirees.

Section IV

The social security administration will be responsible for oversight of this revenue. They will analysis census figures, plus all the new revenue and calculate at what age they can offer full early retirement, raises to retirees and keep social security solvent. Any other use of the revenue will be strictly forbidden and punished by a mandatory 25 to life prison term for any offender.

Chapter 2

This chapter will give you my history and you will see that the only qualifications I have for writing this book is I am an American citizen and have the right to speak my mind. Who am I you may ask. I am just an average citizen. Born and raised in St. Louis and am currently living in Arnold MO just on the outskirts of St. Louis.

In 1964 I graduated somewhere near the bottom of my class at Normandy High School. I was uninspired and immature. I drifted from one menial job to the next. I enrolled in college but was too lazy to do the work. So I quit college and was drafted into the army in 1966. I was trained as a medic and sent to Germany. I served in Germany until 1968 when I was sent back to Fort Dix and received my honorable discharge. It was during this time that I grew up and decided that I wanted to make something of my life. I did not know what, but I became motivated. When I arrived back home, my parents had moved from St. Louis to Arnold, MO. In spite of their move I was able to find them (just kidding. I kept in touch. My parents were kind and wonderful.) I moved back home and drew unemployment for about six months. My father got me a job at American Can Co. factory working on a production line. I knew then that I was not cut out for factory work.

I decided to go back to college. I enrolled at Florissant Valley Community College and then transferred to Meramec Community

College. I needed a purpose in life. It was here that I met my future wife, Pat. This time in college I applied myself and to my surprise, all of a sudden, my grades went up. I started out in business administration, but after taking my prerequisites, I decided that I would rather teach high school (and have my summers off). I transferred to Southeast Missouri State University and graduated with a Bachelor of Science in Secondary Education.

During my college years at Meramec and Southeast MO State Pat and I dated. She transferred to UMSL and graduated with a teaching degree in Spanish and a minor in French. After we both were educated and graduated, we got married on June 23, 1973.

At the time we graduated teaching jobs were hard to find. I was determined and took a job at Salem Jr. High School in Salem, MO. I taught seventh grade social studies and coached M-I basketball. I remember my teaching salary being around $7000 a year and I was paid $500 a year for coaching. My wife got a job working at the local newspaper. She became pregnant with our first child, Mike, and was terminated by the paper. They feared the cost they might incur for her being pregnant.

We had bought a mobile home and had moved it to Salem and that was where we lived. We had joined a bowling league that cost $5.00 a week. We had to quit because we could not afford it. We used my wife's pregnancy as an excuse to but, in reality it was the money and had nothing to do with the pregnancy.

Back in Arnold, my mother had bought a small convenience store and was wanting to retire. She knew we were struggling financially and she offered me the job of running the store. I discussed this with my wife who was homesick as was I. We both decided that we would move back home to Arnold. I began managing the store, we had our first child, Mike, and my wife got a job working for a graphics company as a proofreader. I put in many long hours at the store doing double shifts. I had learned where to buy items and store was doing great. My wife was advancing at the little graphics company that she was part of.

Things were going great and we decided to buy a house. Things went well for a few years. My wife got pregnant and we had our second child, a girl we named Susan. For a few years life was going good. We enrolled our children in a parochial school.

But in our changing world things would start going bad. The store business started to decline as the giant chain store stayed open late and on Sundays. When the blue law in Missouri was repealed it was the kiss of death for small independent stores. For those who do not know what the blue law was I will try to explain it to the best of my ability. Back in the seventies and eighties in Missouri stores that sold certain items could not be open on Sundays. One of the items was 5% beer. If you sold 5% beer you could not be open on Sunday. If you sold 3.2% beer you could be open on Sunday. To top it off, you could not be licensed to sell both. You had to choose between 5% and 3.2% beer. The larger stores opted to sell 5% beer and had to be closed on Sundays and holidays. Small stores that sold 3.2% beer stayed open late and were open on holidays. We sold 3.2% beer, stayed open late and were open on Sundays and holidays, and we did very well.

When the blue law was repealed, it marked the end for many small stores. Now, if you did not sell gas you would have a hard time staying in business. The larger stores now stayed open late and on Sundays and holidays. Everyone sold 5% beer and 3.2% was a thing of the past.

Our store's profits dwindled so I bought a St. Louis Post-Dispatch paper route and delivered papers for a few hours a day while I paid an employee to work at the store. When the paper route was done for the day, I came back and worked in the store till closing. Now I was putting longer and longer hours and making less and less money. I still felt an obligation to make the store work. However, eventually I saw the writing on the wall. I could not compete with the K-marts and Grandpas, and Shop and Saves of the world. Fortunately, my wife had been getting raises and promotions and was now the production manager at her company and was the chief breadwinner in the family. So we were able to keep our house and take vacations.

I had zero self-esteem. My wife asked "Why don't you get a real job?" I started looking for a job and decided that I would give the store back to my mom or close it if she did not want it. She took it back and rented it out for a few months. The renter realized that there was not a profit to be made so he moved out and we closed the store forever.

I had been looking for a job and found a sales job at Best Buy when they opened in St. Louis. I sold my paper route and went to work full time for Best Buy. I went through their training program and started selling appliances. We worked on commission the first couple of years I was there. My coworker, Joy, was our leading appliance salesperson every month. I was always second except for a rare month when I outsold her, but overall she cleaned my clock.

My wife still made more than me, but our combined incomes took a good jump. Now we could afford to take vacations again with our children, and we took them to Disney World twice.

The next change occurred when Best Buy decided to take everyone off of commission. They decided we should all be salaried or hourly. They took the best salesperson from each department and made them the supervisor of that department. The actual title was Senior Appliance Technologist. Their salaries were less than they made on commission, but they were not bad and now they had no pressure to sell. Everyone else was given hourly pay—which was a pay cut for me. I was the second best salesperson in our department. Second best was not good enough. My hourly pay was $7.50. That was a pay cut for me. It was a take it or leave it proposition.

So what do I do now? I have been out of college for 17 years and I still do not have a career. I was very unhappy. I would look for work on a daily basis. That's when I begin to notice all the help wanted ads for nurses. The pay was pretty good and the opportunities seemed to be outstanding. When I told my wife that I wanted to be a nurse she thought I was crazy.

I think part of the reason I wanted to be a nurse had to do with the fact that I had been a medic in the army. I had liked taking care of the sick and injured. My father had lost his circulation in both legs, and he had to have both his legs amputated. I liked taking care of him so I reasoned that if I liked taking care of the ill and liked doing wound care, why not get paid for what I liked doing. I began checking into nursing schools. I decided that I would become an RN rather than an LPN because the pay was better. That was all I knew. I did not know any of the other differences in the two degrees. I would eventually learn that becoming an RN took longer and required you to take on more responsibilities. You also had to learn much more.

I found that at Lutheran Hospital Medical School you could earn an RN degree in two years. By eliminating the summers off, they were able to condense a three year program into two years without cutting any of the content. It would be a grueling program.

I told my wife that I was going to apply, and I called and got the information I needed. At this point even my wife began to take me seriously. I applied and was accepted. I went to school full time and continued to work full time at Best Buy. It was the hardest thing I have ever done. I studied every day. I taped my classes and replayed them on the tape player in the car on my way to and from work. When I got home I studied until I fell asleep every night. I read, studied, and did my clinicals (on job preparation) and through it all I did pretty well in school. The first semester I made all A's, a 4.0 grade point average.

The second semester the questions changed from knowledge questions to situational questions, and my grades began to drop. By the time I graduated my grade point average was just over 3. There were a couple of classes that I was happy to get a C in. Getting one D or F meant that you were out of the program. When I was having a problem I would tell myself "C=RN".

I wasn't the only one having difficulty. We started out with more than 100 students (I think it was 110), and they were all serious and motivated. They all wanted to be nurses. If my memory is correct only 63 graduated. The others failed out.

At Best Buy during my second year of nursing school my friend and supervisor, Joy, informed me on the QT that she would not be allowed to put me on the schedule at Best Buy. Best Buy would not lay me off or fire me, but they could hire others, pay them less and control their schedules. Best Buy did not want to pay unemployment and by taking me off the schedule I would not be eligible for unemployment. I thanked Joy and until this writing had not made this part of my story public. I hold no hard feelings toward Best Buy. They were doing what they felt was right and best for the company.

Since I was now in my second year of nursing school, I was qualified to work in a hospital. I was able to get a job as a nurses assistant and perform jobs such as vital signs, temperatures, pulse, blood pressure and respirations. I could do finger sticks on diabetics. I could do personal care, give showers, turn and reposition patients and do basically anything the RN assigned me. I was actually making more and loving my work.

I graduated in May of 1992 and started my nursing career. I wanted to work in geriatrics and took a job in a nursing home. I started out as charge nurse (this is a nurse that is in charge of a certain wing). He or she makes assignments for the aides, calls the doctors, does treatments and passes meds. I learned to be a treatment nurse. This is a nurse who manages treatment for patients with wounds whether they are bed sores, burns, ulcers of all kinds; but not skin tears. These are usually handled by the CN. I handled the more serious wounds.

I became a supervisor where I evaluated each nurse and aide, acted as a liaison between families and nurses, and was an all around troubleshooter. I also did the hiring and firing of nurses and aides. For a short time I was the acting director of nurses when one got fired and the nursing home was in the process of hiring one. This was a position I never really wanted. In any event I worked very long hours and would stay with an employer about five years.

In December 2005 I took a job as a supervisor at the Woodlands of Arnold Nursing Home where my mother had been placed by my family. My mother now had severe dementia. My father had died in 1992 shortly before I graduated from nursing school. Now that my mother was in a nursing home I would do my job and watch over her care. Her care at the home was excellent. When she passed away, I began questioning whether I wanted to stay as a nursing home supervisor. By this time I had been making almost all the money for our family. Business in the printing industry had dropped off due to home computers and laptops. My wife had quit, been laid off or fired several times and for approximately the last 10 years has stayed at home and let me do the work.

In 2006 my life changed again. On a Friday night, as the Cardinals prepared to win the world series by defeating the Detroit Tigers, I was ready to watch the game on my big screen TV. As I was getting ready to sit down and had a beer ready, my wife got a phone call from her mother's friend. He said he had come to pick up her mother to go dancing, and she had fallen. She couldn't get up and he couldn't help her up because of his heart. My wife told him we would be right over. Her mom lived about 15 minutes away. I assessed her mother. I did a range of motion on her legs and determined that she did not have a fracture. I helped her stand and walked her into the living room. I sat her on the couch. She said that she was not in pain. But she was dirty, her hair was matted and she was a mess. The house was also a mess. It looked like it hadn't been cleaned in years. Her husband had died several years ago. When he was alive the house was always spotless. It was apparent that her mom needed help and was no longer able to take care of herself. This was a revelation. The food in the refrigerator was outdated and her mother could hardly stand on her own. We spent the evening there and I watched the Cardinals win the world series on her little 25" tv.

We put her to bed and then called my wife's three brothers and one sister and left them know what we had found. Everyone had been so busy with their own families that they had not realized the condition of their mother. We took her to the hospital the next morning to have her checked out. They recommended PT and OT at a nursing home. I had her admitted to the Woodlands of Arnold Nursing Home and she went through their PT and OT programs. When she was ready for discharge, we brought her home to live with us and she has been with us ever since. She is able to get around the home on her own. She receives two showers a week and does not need or want for anything. My wife stays home with her on a full time basis and is happy to not have to work.

Meanwhile, by 2007 I was ready for a change in nursing. I gave my supervisor written notice that I would be leaving in 30 days. The nursing director asked where I was going. I told her that I didn't know.

That I was tired of being the supervisor. I wanted and needed more patient care.

This behavior was very unusual for me. Usually when I leave a job, I have another one lined up. This time I was tired of hiring and firing Certified Nurses Aides and just needed a change. I was becoming burned out. The director and I got along very well since the day she was hired and I had helped her during her transitional phase. She told me that I always had a smile and no job was too big for me. She said that she would miss me, but she could see in my face that I needed a change.

A little over a day later the director came back to see me and asked me if I would be interested in hospice work. I told her that it was actually something I was thinking about quite seriously. I think I might enjoy the personal care I could offer in hospice. My director informed me that one of the owners of the Woodlands was also part owner of Alternative Hospice and would like me to interview for a position. I asked the director if she was sure. She said that she was. This surprised me since before I had turned in my resignation, I had called Alternative Hospice, identified myself, and asked about employment. I was informed that there were no positions available. Now they were practically offering me a job. I learned the reason for this during my interview. It is the policy of this hospice not to hire nurses away from the nursing home that they have patients in. Once I turned in my resignation and they spoke with the DON (director of nurses) who gave me a glowing review, I was eligible to be hired.

Funny how things work out. I now have my dream job. I have a career and I make a difference. But America is a mess.

Chapter 3

Now you know who I am and where I came from. You are probably asking yourself what qualifies me to write a book and try to dictate policy in America. To that my answer is that I am not qualified, but what qualified person would write this book? I have a burning desire to write this book. If people read it that would be nice. But regardless of my lack of qualifications, I have to write this book.

On August 20, 2011 I wrote a letter to President Obama explaining that I have a simple, workable plan that would solve the unemployment problem. I told him that it would be an immediate and long term solution. It would stimulate the economy, and he would become one of the most popular presidents ever. I informed him that I had no real qualifications. That I am a college graduate with a nursing degree and that I am not a nut. I also offered to explain a plan that would help with health care and our national debt. As I see it though, the unemployment problem is the easiest to fix and the most urgent. I gave him my phone number and asked him to call me. I mailed the letter on August 20. I started writing this book the next day so I do not know if anything will come from the letter I sent. I am editing the book it is October 8th and I have not heard from the President.

You may wonder what really inspired me to write this book. To that I would say that it wasn't any one thing. It was a multitude of things among them, seeing our country developing into almost a third world country, seeing out health care system having so many shortfalls, for example, the poor denied health care so they learned to go to the hospital emergency room for a runny nose. This causes delays in treating the real emergencies and causes the cost of health care to rise. Seeing people working into their seventies because they can't afford to retire, visiting patients who have worked their whole life and now being denied the health care they need. Seeing our country going through a depression. Seeing our family units turning into single parent families. Seeing so many unemployed Americans. Seeing so many politicians with the morals of alley cats. Seeing the corrupt political system that tears away at our country. The greedy lobbyists and the companies they represent. The inability of our government to function. The soft news our political analysts sell. The fact that nobody is willing to do the right thing. It is no longer about what's good for our country, but how can I get reelected and how much money can I make. The fact someone must offer publicly simple workable solutions to the public if we are to solve our problems. To put it simply, in my America I have a duty to do the right thing. Those are the things that inspired me to write this book. Lets review what we have accomplished in my America. We now have full employment, we now have early full retirement for our seniors, we have a surplus of real jobs, even the poor with little education could get a decent job. The employer would have a smaller base of perspective employees so that is why all citizens would have a shot at real employment. And since the employer would have a larger base of consumers the employer would need to hire more workers and not be so particular. I am not an economist but this sounds to me that this would be good for both the employer and employee. And in turn this would be good for our economy. We have also gained social security that would have a surplus each year. And now we would strive for earlier and earlier full retirement with annual raises. Sounds good.

Chapter 4

So onto our next set of problems health care for all American citizens and paying down our national debt. I am going to tackle these problems together. Because I see the solutions together. In regards to health care let us assume as president Obama has that the rich must pay more. The middle class will pay something less. And the poor will pay something less. But they are all paying their fair share. That makes sense to me. In regards to our national debt lets also agree that the citizens of the United States would like to help. My solutions to both problems are as follows: 1) the government should pass a national sales tax of 2% on every item sold in the united state (including on line purchases) 2) 50% of the revenue generated from this tax should go into an interest bearing account. This money would be used for health care. Every citizen would be issued a card and booklet. The card could be scanned at the doctor's office and or the hospital. The booklet would explain the benefits. In other words the booklet would explain what was covered and was not covered. Also the booklet would let you know where to go for treatment. Where to go for treatment would be determined by the condition your were going to be treated for. This would be regardless of money. For example, life threatening emergencies would be sent to hospital emergency rooms, as they should be. Running noses, colds, rashes and such would be sent to the doctors office. The citizens would have no need for money. There would be no co-pay. There would be no need for health care insurance (as we know it). And there would be no health care premiums to pay. The wealthy will purchase more consumer goods and therefore will pay more for their insurance. The middle class will pay their fair share for health care as will the poor. Each group will purchase what it can afford each month. Health care for all would be accomplished in an fair and equitable way. All citizens would have health care. The cost of health care would go down using this formula. The hospitals would now being used correctly. The doctors offices would now being used correctly. By using the hospitals and doctors offices correctly the cost would be less and the care would be better. So now we would also gain a healthier America. Citizens with health care issues would be free to see doctors of their choice. The fear of paying would be gone. Their care would be better. Lets face it, emergency room doctors do not specialize in nagging health care issues. Usually you are given a temporary fix at the emergency room and sent on your way. With our new health care you would be seeing a doctor that does specialize in long term nagging health care issues. So your course of treatment would be vastly different and far superior at the doctors office.

Conversely, the emergency rooms would be less crowded and true emergencies would be treated better and faster. The response time would be cut and the emergency staff and doctor would be much freer to treat real emergencies. If you went to the wrong place you would be turned away and told to go to the right place. For example, if you walked into the emergency room with a runny nose and elevated temperature the emergency room staff would have you see your primary doctor. This would not be a problem even if you were poor because their would be no cost. As it is now, the emergency room staff would treat you. This would cause delays in treating true emergencies and cause the cost of health care to rise. With our new health care true emergencies would be seen at the hospital emergency rooms and non-emergency conditions would be seen at the doctor's office. These two improvements would create better health care for less money. And our health care would work as it should. Sounds too good to be true doesn't it? Yes, but this is my America.

The other 50% of the revenue generated from this sales tax would go to pay down our national debt. I am still in favor of using any other means to pay our debt down. Cutting fat and waste from our budget is still necessary. As I see it, we borrowed way more money than we had in order to stop our banks from collapsing. Now we must find revenue without the government adding more debt. I would also pass a bill that forbid us from spending more money then we are taking in (balanced budget).

With our new revenue, buzzing economy, early full retirement, new job base, employer and employee working together, health care for all, a dwindling national debt and social security that is not only solvent but has a surplus we are getting to where we need to be in my America. I get carried away at times. Getting back to health care for all and our national debt. So let us assume these measures are put in effect. What are the results? The results are all our citizens now have health care. Emergency rooms are used for emergencies. The poor have basic health care that is just as good as the rich and middle class. I am not an idiot. I realize the rich will be able to pay out of pocket for services not covered by our universal health care. But, that is okay even in my America wealth has it's privileges (not just as much as it does now). We will also have a healthier America. Our national debt will be getting paid down rapidly. How soon will the debt be paid down I cannot calculate (I need more fingers and toes). But in my America we have full employment, early full retirement, health care for all, a healthier and happier America, a surplus in our social security funds and our national debt is being paid down.

These improvements are not free. Let's look at the cost. We have introduced a 2 or 3 % sales tax depending on whether social security needs the 1% tax I talked about. Let's assume for the sake of argument we do need the 1% tax for social security. So now we are at a 3% sales tax on all items purchased in the United States. But, we have eliminated health care premiums. I believe most working Americans pay about $350 a month or $700 a couple per month. I base that believe solely on what I pay. So I could be off, but lets assume I am close. Then we need to take a look at what our different classes would spend in a month to compute how much their health care, social security and our national debt would be costing them. So this is going to be some very rough estimates and examples I am going to use. Let's start with the poor Americans. If the poor Americans are able to spend $1,000 a month on taxable items then 3% of that is $30 a month, so our poor citizens are now paying for their health care a reasonable amount. Lets take a citizen earning $50,000 a year and lets say he spends it all on taxable items. 3% of $50,000 would be $1500 a year or $125 a month. So our middle class citizen would be paying $125 a month for his health care, social security and our national debt. Let's say you make $250,000 a year and you spend $200,000 year on taxable items. Your health care, ss and national debt would be costing you $6,000 a year (3% of $200,000). To pay what our middle class pays for health care now you would have to spend approximately $250,000 a year (3% of $250,000=$7500). So citizens spending in excess of $300,000 a year would start paying their fair share in our health care system. As it is now, the truly poor have no coverage so they go to the emergency room are treated and drive up the cost of health care. The wealthy pay the same as the middle class. So the burden falls on the middle class.

With the new base of collecting from the poor and the truly wealthy paying more we see a more fair and equitable health care system. And since we pay as we go we would have no need for the added cost that health care insurance causes. Remember for health care as it is today, we must pay the cost of health care salesmen, their offices and health care premiums. So our health care cost would go down with everyone paying their fair share.

And our health delivery would be better. As an example, I have talked to patients and have experienced this myself—you go to the emergency room with a true emergency and you sat or lay in the hallway for hours at a time. When I dislocated my shoulder many years ago (playing softball) I laid in the emergency room hallway for 5 hours before I could be seen. I was in terrible pain. One of my patients said that was nothing. He was having a heart attack in the emergency room and he laid in their hallway for 3 hours before he could be seen. He feels as I do he is lucky to be alive. Under this health care system I am proposing true emergencies would be seen very quickly. And nonemergencies would be sent to their doctor's office. Wouldn't it be nice to have health care that worked and covered all American citizens. This health care system would also be more cost effective.

And at the same time we would be paying off our national debt. Having to ask for a sales tax due to our government's inefficiency is not something I like doing. But I prefer that to running our country down and causing a depression. My fear in requesting these sales tax is that our congressmen and women would put this in their general revenue. And they would use these funds for things they were not intended. So we would have to safeguard these funds. We would buy treasury bonds that could only used for their intended purposes. Having said all this I feel we have come a long way in solving our many problems in America. Before I leave the health care issue let me make a few more observations. 1) I applaud president Obama for working toward a universal health care plan and getting it passed. But I have many reservations. 2) has anyone read this monster of a bill (how many pages long is it 1,018)? 3) how does this bill get paid for (if I understand it correctly everyone will be forced to pay some sort of premium) 4) is it really fair and equitable? 5) how are you going to make a poor person pay for something he gets for free now and he says he does not want? 6) how are you going to charge a middle class citizen more than a poor person for the same thing? And how are you going to charge a wealthy person more than a middle class person and more than a poor person for the same thing. Begging will not work.

To better illustrate my point let's say I have a grocery store, and in the grocery store I sell meat, beans and milk (I really specialize). How ridiculous would it be if I had 3 different prices on each item based on what the customer earned in a year. For example, beans sold for 50 cents a can if you earn less than $15,000 a year. Beans sold for 75 cents a can if you earned more than $15,000 a year but less than $100,000 a year. Beans sold for $1.00 a can if you earn more than $100,000 a year. That's got to be the most stupid idea a store could have. Yet, is that what were not selling with the health bill before the American people and sponsored by our president. Lets take the same store and now the beans are 75 cents a can for everybody. There is a 5 cent sales tax on these beans. 3 of the 5 cents goes to social security, health care, and our national debt with each of these entities getting 1 cent a piece. Now the poor person goes in and buys 1 can of beans. By buying these beans he is helping to pay for social security, health care and our national debt. So now a middle class person goes in and buys beans and milk and pays tax on both these products. And now a wealthy person comes in and buys some steak, milk and beans and he pays tax on all these items. All these customers would be helping our social security, health care and national debt. And each set of customers would pay different amounts in helping our social security, national debt and health care. So without all the fuss we would accomplish what we set out to do. Makes sense to me how about you? With the health care system I am advocating no one would be forced to purchase health care. Their would be no health care premiums. The health care booklet would explain what is covered and not covered (much like our policies do now). In addition the booklet would let you know where to go for treatment depending on what you were being treated for. I believe this health care would be more efficient, simpler, cover all American citizens and for the average citizen less expensive. So what's not to like? I don't know. Why is this plan not presented in Congress. I believe because this plan would not make the congressmen and women more money and it would not help their election campaign. I believe the powerful health care lobbyist would hate this plan. Also, I believe our congressmen and congresswomen would hate this plan (after all they receive free health care for life as does their family. Now they would pay for health just like the citizens they represent). Also there would be no special favors from the health care industry to our congressmen and congresswomen. So does this plan have a chance? I don't know, you tell me. Will we take action? Stick around I will get into how to get our congressmen and women's attention later in the book. Here is a sample of my health care bill.

Health care bill number 3215
Section I
Who is covered
The mechanics of the bill / how is it paid for
What is covered
Section II

Who is in charge of the bill

Section III

Exceptions and limitations

Section IV

Hospice/Medicare/Medicaid

Section VI

Review

Section I

1) All Americans citizens at the time of birth are covered. So there are no preexisting conditions to consider. All Americans receive a health care card that can be swiped like a credit card. All approved health care providers will be linked to these health care cards. All Americans will receive a health care card and a handbook at time of birth and all American citizens will be issued the health care cards and handbooks when this health care bill goes into effect. The health care handbook would explain what is covered and where to go for treatment. All medical conditions are covered with the patient or patient's family deciding how aggressive the treatment should be. Education with the doctor and medical team would be an available option for all Americans.

2) The bill is paid for by a 1% sales tax on every item sold in the United States (including online purchases). This revenue would be put into treasury bonds and put into a special health care account. The money in this account can only be used for health care services and will not be put into any general revenue account. Any use of this money other than medical claims will be considered an act of treason and prosecuted as such.

Section II

1) A medical advisory board will be formed and charred by the whip and majority leaders in Washington. They will have equal authority. They will be responsible for investigating claims. All claims will be linked to the internet and only approved health care providers will have this link. The committee will designate state investigators for on sight inspection on any questionable claims.

Section III

1) Limitations and exceptions—Limitations illegal immigrants are not eligible. Exceptions—True medical emergencies, as defined in the health care hand book will be treated for all including illegal immigrants.

Section IV

1) Hospice, Medicare, and Medicaid will not change.

Section V

1) The medical committee will meet every month and review claims, and revenue versus expenditures and make recommendations how to best implement our delivery system.

Here is a sample of our national Dept Reduction bill 33

Section I purpose
Section II how is the bill financed
Section III who has access to the funds and their distribution

Section I

1) The bill is for the express purpose of paying down our national debt

Section II

1) the bill will be financed by a 1% national sales tax on every item sold in the United States (including online purchases)

Section III

1) The United States treasurer and his/her representative will have access to the funds in this sales tax fund that has been created to assist in paying the United States national debt down.

2) The funds from this account will be collected no later than the 5th of the following month and used in the repayment of our National Debt (all other use or uses of this account is strictly prohibited with mandatory prison sentences of 25 years to life for anyone who violates this use).

Chapter 5

Let's now address our dependence on foreign oil and pollution. We will tackle these two together. In my opinion, we need to develop a line of cars that have zero emissions. And these cars have to be affordable, manufactured, and sold. We had just such a car. The car was the EV-1. This car was effectively killed by the California clean air board, the oil companies, our congressmen and congresswomen, and the car manufactures. I believe the reason these cars were killed was because the oil companies feared them, and the others could not make enough money from them. Let me just say I know there are windmills, hydro-power, solar power and so on. But, in my America almost everyone owns a car. And the biggest polluters are the cars. So the problem is how do we get the clean air board, oil companies, our representatives and the car manufactures to do the right thing. That being said, I believe we would need to make cars with zero emissions mandatory. In my America we would pass a clean air bill. The bill would mandate that each car manufacture had to manufacture and sell a certain % of their cars that had zero emissions. For example, year one after passing this bill each car manufacture would have to have 10% of their cars that produced zero emissions. And each year there after another 10% of there cars would have to meet this zero emission standard until 50% of the cars were producing zero emissions. Right now the one car that would fit this need is the electric car. Can you imagine 50% of our new cars being electric? I believe, once people drove these clean hybrid high performance cars they would not want to go back to oil cars. In my America within the next 10 years most cars would be electric cars. The oil burning cars would be becoming obsolete. The obvious advantages of the electric cars are: 1) they are cheaper to operate. You would have to charge the batteries when not being used and/or overnight. This would cost money just like gas and would be just as expensive until gas got over $1.00 a gallon (oops gas is way over a dollar a gallon). 2) they are cleaner to operate. There is no pollution. 3) They are more reliable (there is not as much to break on them). 4) We would no longer be dependent on foreign oil. 5) The environment would be cleaner. 6) It is the right thing to do.

So what are the drawbacks and limitations? Distance you can go without charging your battery is the first limitation or drawback. The second drawback and or limitation is the number of charging stations now available. That is it. Both of these drawbacks or limitations are easily remedied. We have batteries that you can travel 250 miles before needing a charge (although the oil companies now own the patent on these batteries). I am sure others could be developed with minor adjustments that would not infringe on these patents (heck in my America we would force the oil companies to turn the patents over to us as a matter of national security). 2) We would build charging stations next to gas stations since there would be a demand. We might give gas stations an option to add charging stations or not to add them. I believe given this option most stations would opt to have these charging stations. That is all the drawbacks or limitations to having the electric car becoming a viable option to our oil cars.

When I am reading the newspaper usually I get angry. When I read cleaning the environment will cost this country jobs I disagree. If we were making electric cars their would be more jobs. We would have to manufacture the cars. And we would have to build electric charging stations (just like gas stations). I believe cleaning the environment would hurt the oil industry. The oil companies with their powerful lobbyist have successfully fought innovative ideas and killed them. So when I read about trying to save our environment will cost jobs, that makes me think the oil companies are calling all the shots. We started to worry about the environment for many good reasons. But, as time goes by, and our corporations are allowed to cut corners. what happens to the welfare of its citizens? That is a question we should be asking. I think if the jobs cannot be done in an environmental friendly way the jobs should not be considered.

So now in my America we have full employment, a secure social security with a surplus of funds, early full retirement for our seniors (who now can retire early and become great consumers), a stimulated economy, jobs that are not phony, employers and employees working together, a broader base of consumers, health care for all Americans (not only health care but better health care) that is paid for in a fair and equitable way. We have a cleaner environment. We are no longer dependent on foreign oil and our national debt would be dwindling. My Clean air Bill would read:

Reducing dependence on foreign oil and cleaning our environment bill number 5907

I   Forming a clean air board with duties and obligations
II   Limitations, qualifications and salaries
III   0% emissions bill
IV   provisions for charging stations

Section I

1) Each state will have a clean air board. The board will be made up of 5 members. Each member will have an equal vote. And they will pick their own chairman or chairwoman. Their duties will include testing our air quality daily. They will have the power to impose fines, suspend, and terminate licenses for repeat offenders. They also be able to make recommendations and purpose legislation for the citizens to vote on. The board members will meet at least monthly to go over their findings, recommendations and new business. There will be a mandated 0% emission law in place that they will be in charge of enforcing.

Section II

Limitations

No one with ties to manufactures, oil companies, and/or utilities will be allowed to serve on this board. No paid lobbyist will be allowed to contact members of this board. Paid lobbyist will not be allowed to submit proposals or request.

The board members will be paid a salary that is agreed on by the governor of each state not to exceed $75,000 a year. The board members will take a civil servants test before being hired. Veterans will be given a 50 point bonus. The 5 highest scores will be offered these jobs and if someone refuses when offered the next highest scoring person will be offered the job until all the positions are filled.

Section III

0% emission bill

All car manufacturers that sell cars in the United States will have to sell at least 10% of their fleet that produce 0% emissions by 2013. Each ensuing year until 2018 an additional 10% of their fleet must produce 0% emissions. So by 2014, 20% of our cars being manufactured and sold would have 0% emissions, by 2015, 30% of our cars manufactured and sold would have 0% emissions, by 2016, 40% of our cars manufactured and sold would have 0% emissions, and by 2017, 50% of our cars manufactured and sold in the United States would have 0% emissions. Once our cars that had 0% emissions reached 50% in the United States we would be allowed to increase that percentage but never decrease that percentage.

Section IV

Electric charging stations would be able to charge the customers 30% more than what they were paying to the utilities that would service these stations. Charging stations would be allowed at all gas stations.

Chapter 6

So our next challenge is a big one. The challenge is how to make the family unit more normal and the single parent much less desirable in today's society. In my opinion, the family must be more financially rewarded. We must give more incentives to couples who stay together and raise their children. They should be in a lower tax bracket that would allow more than standard deductions for their children. And be given cash rewards if they are truly poor and stay together. We would help with the first 2 children only (we do not want to get into the baby making business that we are currently in now). The qualifications are the parents must live together and they must truly be poor and raise their children together. Them staying together would be easier with all the jobs now available. The reason I am so keen on the two parent model is I think the values of two working parents rubs off on their children. I believe this school of hard work makes better citizens down the road. This type of environment would do much to eliminate the undesirable members of society (such as the druggies and the gang members). I believe, this type of environment would make America a better place to live.

We must slow down the rewards for unmarried mothers. When aide to dependent children was adopted the parent (usually the mother) received aide from the government for the first 18 years of the child's life. This was overhauled and reduced to the first 5 years of the child's life in 1996 by a bill signed off by President Clinton. Now some girls begin having babies every year for 5 years in a row and this becomes their full time job. Following this logic you are financially rewarded by becoming a baby factory. But this also makes you a one parent family your partner is not allowed to help you raise these children. So in essence our government has created a welfare society and hurt our economy and the children being born into this welfare state. This is just wrong. The children are raised and do not receive proper parenting, do not have male role models and many turn to life on the streets. They become gang members as a way to belong to a family. Their morals are poor, life is cheap, drugs are plentiful and hope for a better life nonexistent.

It is time to overhaul this welfare system. In my America it would be more financially rewarding for families to stay together. With cash rewards being given to poor families who stay together and raise their children. When this happens better examples are set for the children in their early years and they in turn strive to have good morals and a good work ethic like their parents. So now we have created a working environment and have discouraged a welfare society. In my America jobs are plentiful regardless of your education or background so now men and women can get a decent paycheck. When this happens a working environment is created. I believe, with this working environment accompanied by 2 parent families you have great role models for their children. It would now be unprofitable to have babies out of wedlock. The family would be more important. I believe with both parents working and raising their children the odds are the children will become more productive citizens. The family values will be more directed toward hard work equals achievement. The parents will want their children to have more education and better jobs than they had. Conversely the gang environment will become less important. The government's involvement will be reduced as these children grow up with a sense of hard work. These children will aspire to better education and be more productive citizens. You realize this approach would lead to less poor people. Our population would become more affluent.

I am not heartless. I would grandfather in existing welfare. But, I would change any new welfare. I feels girls and guys are going to make mistakes and the baby should not have to pay for these mistakes (after all this is America). But, I also feel they should learn from these mistakes. So I would continue to offer assistance to unwed mothers with one child. But, along with assistance would be education (which would include free contraceptives thru our national health care system). If an unwed mother had a second child out of wedlock there would be no additional funds from our government. She could get assistance from her family or give the child up for adoption. So low income parents who stayed together the government would help with 2 children and 1 parent families would receive assistance for one child only.

This would not be popular but needs to be done. The reasons are many but I believe we need to move government out of family business. By instilling the hard work, raise your children virtues; I believe poverty and crime would go way down. I also believe we would be helping our citizens as we should be. So getting the government out of family business is a good thing. Since most parents are pushing their children to do better than they did we would have an ever changing society. We would be increasing our productive citizens and our middle class would be growing. Our poor would be dwindling. This would be a more ambitious America. The druggies, gangs, and hopeless parts of society would be dwindling. And all these changes are good. Very soon the government involvement in families would be very small. The first time unwed mothers would have support and not become baby factories. Because of the education they would be offered they would not have more babies out of wedlock. Since there is free contraceptives available thru our national health care the amount of babies being born to unwed mothers should go down.

Here is a sample of my Aide to Dependent Children Amendment: ADC Aide to Dependent Children Amendment

I Who is eligible:

1) One parent families and two parent families
2) How the benefits now differ for one parent families and two parent families

One parent families that earn less than what considered the current poverty level will be eligible for $3,500 assistance from social security annually for the first 5 years of their first child's life. Any children beyond the first born to a one parent family will not eligible for any additional benefits.

Two parent families that stay together and raise their children and earn less than the current poverty level will be eligible for $3,500 annually from social security for the first 10 years of their first two children's life. ($7,000 a year maximum). No additional money will be rewarded for more than 2 children. If during this period the two parent families rises above the poverty level the government will continue these subsidies. For the entire 10 years. All families are eligible for free contraceptives and sex education as provided by our national health care.

As I see it, in my America we have solved many problems. Starting with unemployment—we now have full employment with real jobs. Our social security would be secure. We would have early full retirement for our seniors. We would have a large base of working

Americans. We would have younger retirees that would help stimulate our economy. We would not be adding phony jobs. We would have health care for all American citizens. The health care would be paid for in a fair and equitable way. Our national debt would be dwindling. We would no longer be dependent on foreign oil. We would have a cleaner environment. We would have a healthier society. Our social security system would have a surplus. Our two parent families would become the norm. We would have reworked family values. We would have gotten the poor back into the mainstream. We would have reduced the need for a society with gangs. A better lifestyle would be developed for most of our citizens. Welfare would be reduced. Our children would be more ambitious overall.

We have not tackled the politicians. Before I do that I would like us to look back in our history. I would like to look at some of the wars in which we have fought. I would like to look at our current politicians and see what we are really getting for our money. I will offer you the citizen a chance to offer your opinion loud and clear. And I believe we will get the politicians attention. But, for now I need to remind you of an old joke I once heard. There is a reason I am telling you this funny. So here goes. A young man was in a covered wagon that was being pulled by a mule. When the young man came to a bridge the mule looked around and refused to pull the wagon across the bridge. The young man pulled at the mule, begged the mule and gave the mule treats but to no avail. The mule would not budge. An old man was watching when the young man said I would give anything to get that mule to pull my wagon across that bridge. The old man told the young man for $5 I will get that mule to pull your wagon over that bridge in no time. The young man could not believe this. So he pulled out a 5 dollar bill gave it to the old man and said here is your $5 now lets see you get that mule across that bridge big mouth. The old man picked up a 2x4 board and smacked the mule right between the eyes with this board. The old man then boarded the wagon and pulled the reins and told the mule to giddy up and the mule proceeded to pull the wagon across the bridge. The young man met the old man on the other side of the bridge and asked him how did he do that? The old man told the young man before you can get the mule to do anything you first must get his attention.

That is exactly how I feel about our politicians. Stick around, get your 2x4's ready and I will give you a way to get the politicians attention. We have fought in many wars and I feel we are in a war that reminds me of the Revolutionary and Civil War. In the Revolutionary war we had the intolerable acts by the British. In this war I believe, we have the intolerable inaction by our representatives. In the Civil war the fight was strictly in America. Those are some of the reasons I have picked those two wars to look back on. I see many correlations and comparisons in what our forefathers went thru in the colonies and what we are facing today. The differences are the enemy was easy to see. The wrongs were done out in the open and were easy to see. I believe, theses wrongs are harder to find. And the worst tyranny is the omissions in solving America's problems. I believe, our politicians are having a party 24/7. They don't have to worry about the things we the people are facing every day. And for the most part they don't worry about those things. They give lip service as if they do. But, for the most part I do not think they care. Do I think all politicians are evil? No I don't, they just need to be shown the way. And like the mule we first have to get their attention. Do I think all politicians should be voted out of office in 2012? Yes I do, I believe the good with bad should all be voted out of office. It is what we need to do to get the politicians attentions. We need to save America and make America better. That is what our forefathers did. They informed the British they were tired of the bullshit and they were not going to take it anymore. We need to inform our representatives that we are tired of the bullshit and we are not going to take it anymore. So lets look back in history I have copied some interesting tidbits for us to look at and here they are. The American Revolutionary War (from the free Wikipedia encyclopedia)

The American Revolutionary War (1775-1783) or American War of Independence, or Simply Revolutionary War, began as a war between the Kingdom of Great Britain and the thirteen British colonies of North America and ended in a global war between several European great powers.

The war was the result of the political American Revolution, which galvanized around the dispute between the Parliament of Great Britain and colonist opposed to the Stamp Act of 1765, which the Americans protested as unconstitutional. The parliament insisted on its right to tax colonist; the Americans claimed their right as Englishmen to no taxation without representation. The Americans formed a unifying Continental Congress and a shadow government in each colony. The American boycott of British tea led to the Boston Tea Party in 1773. London responded by ending self government in Massachusetts and putting it under the control of the army with General Thomas Gage as governor. In April of 1775 Gage sent a contingent of troops out of Boston to seize rebel arms. Local militia know as 'minutemen' confronted the British and nearly destroyed the British column. The Battles of Lexington and Concord ignited the war. Any chance of compromise ended when the colonies declared independence and formed a new nation, the United States of America on July 4, 1776.

France, Spain and the Dutch Republic all secretly provided supplies, ammunition and weapons to the revolutionaries starting in early 1776. After early British success, the war became a standoff. The British used their naval superiority to capture and occupy American coastal cities while the rebels largely controlled the countryside, where 90% of the population lived. British strategy relied on mobilizing Loyalist militia, and was never fully realized. A British invasion of Canada ended in the capture of the British army at the Battle of Saratoga in 1777. That American victory persuaded France to enter the war openly in early 1778, balancing the sides military strength. Spain and the Dutch Republic—French allies—also went to war against Britain over the next two years, threatening an invasion of Great Britain and severely testing British strength with campaigns in Europe. Spain's involvement culminated in the expulsion of British armies in West Florida, securing the American southern flank.

French involvement proved decisive yet expensive as it ruined France's economy. A French naval victory in the Chesapeake forced a second British army to surrender at the Siege of Yorktown in 1781. In 1783 the Treaty of Paris ended the war and recognized the sovereignty of the United States over the territory bounded roughly by what is now Canada to the north, Florida to the south, and the Mississippi River to the west.

The Declaration of Independence was a statement adopted by the Continental Congress which announced that the thirteen colonies, who were at war with Great Britain, declared themselves as free independent states. Thomas Jefferson was the author of this document and it was very eloquent. The following sentence is highly regarded as one of the best sentences ever written by many scholars: We hold these truths to be self-evident, that all men are created equal, that they are endowed by their creator with certain unalienable rights, that among these are life, liberty and the pursuit of happiness. That sentence pretty much says it all. I believe, our current politicians are not attempting to follow those guidelines and that is one of the main reasons I wrote this book. I am humbled by such great men as Thomas Jefferson. And such a great document as the Declaration of Independence. Jefferson was such an eloquent writer and when he writes about our unalienable rights: right to life, liberty and the pursuit of happiness I can't help but wonder what would he think of a no action congress like we are stuck with. Of a government that is no longer doing the right things for its citizens they are governing. The question I keep coming back to is: are we at a point where we need to dissolve our political system? And I don't believe we are at that point. I think the system could work. I believe we are at a point where we need to get rid of our political leaders.

When Jefferson talks about how government gets its powers from the masses I no longer believe that to be the case. Our government gets elected by the masses but its powers are derived from the political lobbyist. I believe, if Jefferson could see what is happening in our government today he would be shocked and ashamed. Jefferson I believe, would want these politicians booted out of office. He might advocate taking up arms as a way of getting rid of these politicians. In our forefather's revolution Intolerable acts were often used and became one of the main reasons we declared our independence. Those acts were intended to raise money for Great Britain and if they hurt the colonies, well too bad. When the colonies ignored these acts or refused to follow them Great Britain attempted to force them to follow these acts. When Great Britain failed at forcing the colonies to follow these acts Great Britain initiated acts that were meant to punish the colonies and force the colonies to accept Great Britain as their masters. This lead to more defiance by the colonies and eventually war. I believe, what we have today is Intolerable inaction of our representatives. I believe, for the most part, our representatives are now representing themselves and the lobbyist they work for. I believe it is time for our revolution. Our revolution would be fought by the American people using modern day technology as their weapons. We would get into contact with our representatives by e-mail, twitter, facebook, their own web sites, writing letters and so on (any means available). We would list our demands and solutions and when nothing happened we would vote these representatives out of office. Back in time the American people took up their muskets, fought the British and formed our United States of America. We need to take up our arms, contact our representatives, and then vote them out of office. I included a little of the Civil War because it was fought entirely in America by Americans. And the war we need to wage is now in America and will be strictly fought by Americans.

American Civil War from Wikipedia, the free encyclopedia

The American Civil War (1861-1865) was a civil war in the United States of America. Eleven Southern states declared their secession from the United States and formed the Confederate States of America to fight for independence. Twenty (mostly northern states) free states in which slavery had already been abolished and five states known as boarder supported the federal government. These twenty-five states were referred to as the Union states, they had a much larger population base and more industry than the South. After four years of war the South surrendered and secession from the union and slavery were outlawed.

Once again we showed this ability to stand up and fight for what we believe in. Abraham Lincoln was not a well-liked president in his time. But he stood up for what he thought was right and only for the sake of this being right for our country. It would have been easier to let the South secede or keep slavery or both. But it would have been wrong in his eyes. Lincoln then delivered the Gettysburg Address shortly after the Battle of Gettysburg. It is one of the greatest speeches ever given and showed his true feelings. I have copied it for you for a reason that you will see after reading this address.

"Four score and seven years ago our fathers brought forth on this continent a new nation, conceived in liberty, and dedicated to the proposition that all men are created equal.

Now we are engaged in a great civil war, testing whether that nation or any nation, so conceived and so dedicated, can long endure. We are met on the battle-field of that war. We have come to dedicate a portion of that field, as a final resting place for those who here gave their lives that the nation might live. It is altogether fitting and proper we should do this.

But in a larger sense, we can not dedicate, we can not consecrate, we can not hollow this ground. The brave men, living and dead, who struggled here, have consecrated it, far above our poor power to add or detract. The world will little note, nor long remember what we say here, but it can never forget what they did here. It is for us the living, rather, to be dedicated here to the unfinished work which they who fought here have thus far so nobly advanced, it is rather for us to be here dedicated to the great task remaining before us—that from these honored dead we take increased devotion to that cause for which they gave their last full measure of devotion—that we here highly resolve that these dead shall not have died in vain—that this nation, under God, shall have a new birth of freedom—and that government of the people, by the people, for the people, shall not perish from the earth."

Wow, what a speech. Are we still a government of the people, by the people and for the people or has this type of government perished? That is my question. Are we now a government of the wealthy politicians, by these politicians, for their lobbyist.? Do we need a change? You bet! I have done my best to present how we could change America and I hope and pray that enough others read my book and take up action as I have described.

I found that reviewing our revolutionary history/war and our civil war most fascinating and necessary. I feel we are now ready to have our revolution. If we are to solve our problems we need to be just as determined as our forefathers were. We need to have has much guts as they did. We need to be ready to fight for the right things. The hard part is to identify the enemy. I truly believe the enemies are our current bred of politicians. Unlike our forefathers who made hard decisions because they were the right thing to do these scoundrels base their decisions on two things and for the most part only two things. I believe, the two things these politicians base their decisions on are will this plan or bill make me more money and/or will this plan or bill help my reelection campaign. Unlike our forefathers who were drafted into service and served their country and then went back into their civilian occupation these politicians are life long hangers on and stay most of their lives on a party scholarship. Our forefathers were not hangers on and did not have the amount of lobbyist we have today. I feel our politicians of today are greatly influenced by these lobbyist. I believe our current politicians could care less about the citizens they are suppose to be representing. And therefore are not interested in really fixing the real problems most Americans are facing today.

My solution is to start our revolution by getting rid of all incumbent politicians. And make our politicians know they are not on a party scholarship. They are in Washington to serve our citizens. They need to have a game plan. We need to get their attention. Remember the mule. Get your 2x4's ready.

When is the last time we felt like our politicians had our back? I am hoping with our fighting spirit we will change the course of history. In the conclusion of this part, will we have formed a "more perfect union" or will it be business as usual? Remember the preamble to our constitution? "We the people of the United States in order to form a more perfect union, establish justice, insure domestic tranquility, provide for the common defense, promote the general welfare, and secure the blessings of liberty to ourselves and our posterity, do ordain and establish this constitution for the United States of America." Wow what a document! After revisiting our past I see citizens who were courageous and fighters. I feel we have the greatest fight we have ever fought ahead of us. The odds are stacked against us (sort of like David and three Goliaths). The three Goliaths I refer to are our elected officials. The congressmen and congresswomen, senators, and our president will be formidable adversaries. If America is worth saving, and I believe it is, then we as citizens are going to have to take control of these politicians. The question is how?

Remember the mule crossing the bridge? The first thing we must do is get their attention. And the way we do that is contact them by any means we can. Be prepared the first time we get in touch with them to see no real results (action). So the second step we must take is to vote all incumbents out of office. What if in 2012's election every incumbent lost his or her job. Can you imagine the message that would send? So now we make contact with the newly elected politicians and they will take us seriously when we tell them why they were elected. We would also have shown these politicians we are not afraid to use our 2x4's. When we get in contact with these newly elected officials we would let them know that the same fate awaits them if they do not do their jobs and start representing the masses. As part of their jobs we want to know at least two things: 1) what do they plan to do to make America better, how they plan to do this and when will it get accomplished. 2) what do they plan to do to make their local communities better, how they plan to do this and when will it get accomplished.

That's right. I believe, our politicians should be required to have a game plan (just like teachers have lesson plans and nurses have care plans). If they do not have a game plan that they implement they will not be re-elected. You know when you are being watched by the boss you will work. We should be the bosses and these politicians should be striving to make America a better place for the masses. If they are only interested in making more money for themselves and serving the lobbyist who bribe them and the wealthiest Americans they will not be re-elected. We will submit our plans on how to fix employment, social security, health care, national debt, family units, dependence on foreign oil, our environment, our welfare system and so on. And we will expect an answer and action to go along with the answer. So now the politician's future would actually be based on performance.

After rereading this book, I now know that what I was trying to say in a simple way is that we the masses must become our own lobbyist. The politician's future will now depend on their job performance (like all other Americans). One of the things we should demand is a yearly evaluation of these politicians (after a year in office we need to see what they have accomplished). Can you imagine working for a year and not being able to show your boss what you have accomplished? So wanting to see our employee's work should not be a problem. I would also like to see their attendance record.

Since we are the bosses we should demand no bills be over three pages in length. The bills must stand on their own. No earmarks allowed. The language in the bills must be plain and straight forward. So that the average American citizen could read these bills and understand them. This is America and we the citizens are taking it back. This will be harder than any war we have fought. I believe these career politicians are used to the shell game and are masters of deception. We must get their attention and keep them focused. They will continue to fleece us for as long as we allow them to do so. We must be diligent and demand to see their work. How many days did they attend congressional sessions? What bills did they sponsor that became law? I don't believe this is too much to demand. The politicians want us to grade our teachers. So wouldn't the politicians being graded be a good idea?

When our current politicians make a speech now don't believe them. I believe that just because a politician states something now has no bearing on the truth. Make them prove everything and put everything in writing. I believe, the idea of life long, do nothing politicians (but get laid as much as possible and collect bribes from lobbyist) should end in 2012. And this could happen if there are enough David's out there. Get your sling shots, letters, emails, twitters, faxes, facebook and whatever means of communication ready.

Right now, I believe our politicians are doing this country many disservices. When they cannot work together to fix the problems I talked about in this book then they should not be in office. I believe, some of the more distasteful things I have witnessed by our politicians are: 1) the way they roll out our soldiers praise them and act like they care. In my opinion they really don't care about these soldiers. When you see unemployed military service men begging, unable to find work; and these politicians doing nothing, what other conclusion could you draw? I believe when these politicians are praising the soldiers and telling them how much they appreciated their service what they are really concerned with is how showing these soldiers will help their re-election. The politicians may act sincere but I believe they are not. I call this example lets dupe the American people with parading a soldier.

In my dreams I think of our politicians as ring masters in a circus. They see the citizens as so many dopes. When they parade a soldier I think of them as acting like Jerry Lewis in his telethon. The soldiers are begging for money and the lines are lighting up (but in this case the lines don't light up). And I don't believe they care. They want it to appear that they care. An example of parading (using) a soldier can be found in the Pat Tillman story.

Remember Pat Tillman, pro football player, who enrolled in the army as an enlisted man. He was killed by friendly fire. Our military and politicians covered this up and planted a story that he was killed in action while saving some of our soldiers and fighting the Taliban. Pat Tillman was awarded the Sliver Star. But Pat's family was inquisitive and pressed to find details. And they found the cover up. The Tillman family had so much integrity that our government didn't know what to do. Eventually they had to admit they had made the whole story up. So then they tried to blame the whole cover up on a one star retired general. When another document showed the cover up went way up the chain of command they went to a grand jury. The grand jury treated the people who testified very friendly and took all their explanations at face value. So the cover up was accomplished and it's really a shame because all the Tillman family wanted was the truth. So when I say don't believe our politicians there are very good reasons.

Another example of our politicians doing more harm than good happens in the Afro-American communities. In these communities there is a great deal of unemployment (especially with the males). Using my formula we would have these males working with real jobs and benefits. Their self esteem would be going up. The children would have a two parent model more than they do now. But instead I believe our politicians offer meaningless temporary jobs or phony jobs. These jobs do more harm than good. They add to our increasing debt and have no lasting effect on the community. If real jobs were plentiful there would be more hope, more assimilation, a better lifestyle and less gangs and/or druggies. I see the politicians in this script as W C Fields when he says "Never give a sucker an even break". And our politicians really adhere to this line and do not give these people an even break.

In my last example I see the citizens of Jefferson County where I live there are many puppy mills and meth labs. These are the jobs that they are raised into. I believe if there were plentiful jobs that had benefits and you could take pride, in most of these puppy mills and drug houses would close. And our citizens would become much more productive. One parent families exist in both these communities and continue to be a problem for the children, families and our government. I believe, this problem would all but go away if my solutions were followed. What have we got to lose? The last group I see as dog trainers in a circus. The ring masters are the politicians who crack the whip on these trainers.

You know I have a sense of humor but I am not laughing. These are sad commentaries on today's America. But I believe in order to change these commentaries we must change our cultural norms. Right now I believe the cultural norms are: 1) we complain about our politicians but we take little action 2) we have no plan of action so things go on as they have. I believe, we keep incompetent scoundrels in office representing us. I believe, we don't make our politicians accountable because we do not have a game plan. We now have a game plan. Contact your representatives and when nothing happens vote them out of office. I know this is a simple game plan. But, I believe the simpler the better. When plans get too involved nothing really happens. I believe, our game plan should never be longer than three items (two is better). If you accomplish the two things on your game plan then do another short game plan. Like on the candy kiss (keep it simple stupid). When you do that you will be amazed at how much you can accomplish.

Some of my ideas I have expressed in more concrete terms than others. But, I have kept my game plan simple. So you can decide whether you are with me or against me. Whether you agree or disagree.

The main thing I want you to think about in my game plan is is it workable? Can we as Americans actually pull this off? I do not expect this to be easy. We would have to allow for a few minutes everyday to work on our problems. To go to the polls to cast your ballots. To pick up your 2x4's. To get your sling shots and slay the three goliaths we are facing.

Remember the wars we have fought in, the lives we have lost fighting for our country. Remember our unalienable rights (life, liberty and the pursuit of happiness). Are we going to let our politicians rob us of these rights? It is too late for the me to retire early I will be 66 in May. And I will be eligible for full retirement then. But, it is not too late for my son or daughter. Think of what you can do for your children. Or yourself if your young enough to benefit from early retirement.

Think about all the things I have written in this book. Are you still thinking? Are you still thinking? Are you still thinking? Now imagine it is five years later and all the things we talked about have come to pass. We have full employment. The economy is booming. Age 60 is now the full retirement age. Our health care is the best in the world. Everyone chooses their doctor and their are no health care premiums. Our young seniors are spending their money right and left. The employers are making lots of money. But, they could make more if they could find more workers. Americans are enjoying more time with their families. Almost all children have 2 parents raising them. And the children now have a great work ethic. There are so few people addicted to drugs that you can't make a living selling them. Gang cultures have been replaced by family cultures. Our politicians are submitting game plans for the good of the masses. Bills are no longer than three pages and there are no add ons or earmarks. Our environment is getting cleaner and less polluted. We are no longer dependent on foreign oil. 50% of our cars are electric and the oil cars are no longer in demand. Americans have found out how superior the electric cars are. We have batteries that can travel 500 miles before needing a charge. We have as many charging stations as gas stations. Can you imagine all that? I remember a great quote from Methuseiah II You see things; and you say "why"? But I dream things that never were; and I say "Why not"?

That quote struck a cord with me and many Americans. And I believe to this day that is what we should be thinking. Another quote I keep thinking of when writing this book is the one from Martin Luther King "I have a dream." I know there is more to the quote than that but, I have not been to the mountain yet. But I do have a dream and that dream is that the problems I have mentioned in this book would all be fixed. And I would live long enough to see this.

I do not think of myself as a rebel. But a rebel is not necessarily a bad thing. Our forefathers had some real rebels with great quotes. Remember who said "I only regret that I have but one live to loose for my country". (Nathan Hale right before the British hanged him), who said "Give me liberty or give me death". (Patrick Henry). I am as patriotic as any one. When a concert ends with an uplifting flag waving song I am standing singing and holding back the tears. That does not make me a pushover. I believe the wrongs that are now being done in our America by the people we have elected are intolerable. I have worked most of my adult life so I believe in the virtue of hard work. But, when I read about so many young Americans that have lost their jobs I say this is wrong. This is America the land of opportunity. I believe our elected officials have not come up with any plans that would truly decrease the number of unemployed. I wonder why they are drawing a paycheck. I believe they are either incompetent, lazy and/ or apathetic. But, really maybe none of those terms apply. Maybe they figure full employment will not make them more money or help their election campaign (So why bother)?

Chapter 7

Many people will view my ideas as radical, extremist or unamerican. I say nothing could be further from the truth. What is radical wanting a better America? What is radical about wanting full employment? What is radical about wanting a secure social security that also has a surplus of funds in it? What is radical about jobs being so plentiful that all Americans have a shot at the American dream? What is radical about an America where early retirement is accepted and is a goal of our political leaders? What is radical about employers and employees needing each other and working together? What is radical about two parent families becoming the norm? What is radical about getting the government out of family business? What is radical about not allowing the government to spend money we don't have on things we don't need? What is radical about not letting the government supply phony temporary jobs that do more harm than good and are very costly? What is radical about protecting our environment? What is radical about ending our dependence on foreign oil? What is radical about health care for all Americans? What is radical about a health care system being more efficient? What is radical about a balanced budget? What is radical about our national debt being paid down? What is radical about bills we understand?

I could ask these same questions about being an extremist. I am not a radical or an extremist. I am mainstream. I only see one of my ideas as radical. That radical idea is that we take control of our elected officials. We no longer accept their incompetence, laziness, being corrupt and apathetic. We flood them with correspondence. We get their attention. Yes, I believe this is a radical idea. I also believe making each elected official submit a game plan and being graded on that game plan is a radical idea. That being said, I don't think taking control of our elected officials and making them submit a game plan is a bad idea. I think the powers that be may attack my plans as being socialistic. And to a point they are socialistic ideas. The rich would be contributing more for the greater good of the poor and middle class. So there is some validity to that criticism. On the other hand every American would be paying their fair share. We would be getting the government out of family business.

Other critics may say I glossed over my plans and there is little depth to them. My response is my bills would be straight forward and less than 3 pages in length and they would work. I would not allow add ons to any bills. I would outlaw paid lobbyist. My health care bill would be simple, easily paid for and cover every American. Social security would be solvent and paid for in a more equitable manor. The real problem with my solutions are they would not make our politicians more money nor would they help their election campaigns. And they would not help their wealthiest friends. We would no longer be paying more for our heath care premiums each year and receiving less coverage each year (as we do now). And I don't think a limited amount of socialism is a bad thing. Our policemen and fireman are based on the greatest good for greatest number of people. And I certainly think we need them and I am happy to keep them. The military is also an example of the greatest good for the greatest number of people. I think my biggest critics will be the politicians, our corporations and their lobbyist. I say nuts to them. I don't care. I am supporting the masses of Americans who have fought and died for this country. So I am not too concerned about any of my critics. I am open to all other ideas but, ideas without a plan of action are worthless. So, as I keep saying, get your 2x4's and sling shots ready. We need to get some political attention. We need to start a peaceful revolution. I believe if we do nothing more than vote all the incumbents out of office in 2012 we will have gotten the politician's attention.

When we declared our independence from Great Britain we had to endure many unfair acts. In this book I hope we are declaring our independence from our politicians. That we are now taking a more active role in our government. Really, with our mass media and technical advantages we should be more active in controlling these politicians. In my America there is much cultural differences among its people. And that is what makes this country so interesting. But, there is a common dream, raising a family, having a career or job that you can be proud of, making enough money to live a good lifestyle—new car, vacations, money in the bank, and your children doing better than we did. Right now that dream is not happening for many and it is very sad.

Chapter 8

My problems in writing this book are: 1) I am not a writer 2) I say things as I see them 3) how do I keep my book as long as a girls skirt 4) my vocabulary does not allow me to use really intelligent sounding words 5) laziness 6) I am technology challenged. So you see I had a lot of limitations in writing this book. But it needed to be written if for no other reason than I had to get my thoughts and feelings into print. These ideas are all mine as far as I know. I came up with these ideas when reading the newspapers and watching the news on tv. I am sure there are others out there that have good ideas. In any event in this day of mass media wouldn't it be great if we changed America for the better using all of our technology. I am so technology challenged that my wife had to set up the computer and link the text blocks from one page to the next. My wife programmed my cell phone, my daughter programmed my mp3 player, and my son is in control of the remotes at home (sometimes I cannot figure how to turn the tv on). My wife also proofread this book before we printed it.

Other limitations, I am old 65 at this writing. I have a hard time expressing my thoughts. So for me to actually write a book is against all odds. In this age of technology I am a dinosaur. The one thing I have going is I think in concrete terms and address our problems as if they were a nursing care plan. Problems I notice when I am watching the news, CNN, reading newspapers, and watching special political reports are: 1) the softness of the interviewer. I am amazed at how many questions that are directed toward someone getting elected. I think please ask them to show you their game plan. Ask them to show you how many bills they have sponsored to make America better. Ask them how they plan on eliminating unemployment, fixing social security, fixing our health care, fixing our national debt problems and so on and so forth. I don't care about their election campaign. I don't care to hear them criticize someone else. If they were doing their jobs, everything I wrote about in this book would be fixed.

That was a real tantrum, but it needed to be said. These political analyst need to start thinking outside the box. They need to start representing the American people. I realize their sponsors are not going to stand for that too much. But, there has to be a few David's left in broadcasting doesn't there? It irks me to high heaven that our teachers and nurses make up workable lesson plans and care plans and our politicians do not make up workable plans to make America better for the masses for whom they are supposed to be working. This must change if we are to make America a better place to live and die in. When our preamble to our constitution talks about a "more perfect union" it is referring to keeping the United States together and making the United States a better place to live. I think these sentiments still ring true. We need to work at making America better period. As I see it we can be part of the solution or part of the problem I believe, as it is now our biggest problem is our current politicians and their current value system. Remember my axiom. I believe, that our politicians are only concerned about two things: 1) how to make more money and 2) how to help their election campaign.

Our current citizens are too passive and/or apathetic. We the citizens need to change first if we are to have any hope of changing our politicians. This will be our biggest battle giving lip service will not cut it. We need to take up arms and serve our country now. Americans have fought in wars to preserve our lifestyle. We Americans are natural born fighters. We also are natural born fixer uppers. Get the hammer, nails, screwdrivers, screws and duct tape out. We need our politicians to be just as good at fixing things as we are.

I have another story to illustrate this point. This time the story happens to be true. This summer it was very hot in St. Louis with many days over 100 degrees. One of my patient's air conditioner was going out. The patient did not have any money for a new air conditioner. This happened on a Tuesday evening. The family had called Cool Down St. Louis, a group sponsored to help the poor in these types of crises. But, Cool Down St. Louis was overwhelmed and they were not taking any applications. So I called our social worker and we decided to add this problem to the patient's care plan on Wednesday. At the Wednesday meeting I brought this problem to light. And wouldn't you know it, we had just gotten a window unit back that we had loaned a family during their time of need. It was suggested we take this unit to my patient's house. Everyone agreed. We added it his care plan. As things worked out, I had been on call the night before and was going on no sleep. Our social worker along with one of our nurses and her teenage son took the air conditioner to our family in need. Our social worker called me that evening and told me they got the air conditioner down there and had a police officer help them put it in the patient's window. She told me she thought it went pretty well and they secured the unit using duct tape. I went to my patient's house with 2x4's and tools in hand and finished securing the unit. The family still has the unit, the house is cool, and we solved my patient's problem within 24 hours. I know the government cannot solve our problems that quickly but it should be one of its goals to solve our problems as quickly as possible. Instead I get the feeling their goals are to do as little as possible, make as much money as possible, and take on as little responsibility as possible. And for our elected officials that is unacceptable.

Chapter 9

I read about these special taxes for special projects but, I don't see us fixing mainstream America. But, I believe we know why these special projects that lead to special taxes are so popular. Special projects lead to special favors and that is just the way it is, and we don't like it. I believe, special projects and taxes to fund these projects are great for our politicians. The politicians look like they care. When we have a natural disaster like a hurricane or a tornado the politicians come, look and authorize special funding. This helps their image. They are able to add some temporary jobs and now their election campaign is helped. They are now able to show how they helped these citizens.

That is great because in a crises we should help our citizens. But, the problem is mainstream America is in crises with our health care, unemployment, social security, national debt, welfare, environmental and political system. We don't fix these, we he haw around instead. I believe, for the most part, these politicians are greedy and uncaring and that is why our problems are not fixed. When I read our stimulus package that include proposals to add monies for the repair of our roads, bridges, schools and airports I cringe at the thought of this. These are just the type of proposals that do more harm than good. Temporary phony jobs fix nothing. I also would like to know where has the money for bridges and roads gone? With each gallon of gas we buy a certain percentage goes to repairing our roads and bridges so why are they soliciting funds for these? Why are we adding to our national debt for these? Where has our gas tax money gone? School and airports are usually supported on a state level. We continue to pass taxes for these. So where has that money gone? Giving the schools and airports a hand I could live with but how is that really helping unemployment?

Another issue I have is why are we poisoning our environment by abandoning stricter emission rules. We should be doing just the opposite. We should demand a cleaner environment. We give lip service to fighting cancer. But, I believe some forms of cancer are related to our environmental issues. I know we could reduce unemployment if more of us contracted cancer and died. But, I don't think that type of full employment plan is acceptable. It just seems to me there is no common sense left in Washington. The plans I outlined would solve our problems without an 800 billion dollar stimulus package. We should be encouraging early retirement and a cleaner environment. I believe, if common sense were dynamite our leaders couldn't blow their noses. As far as the detractors of social security, I say nuts to you. Many of our Americans have fought for this country and now rely on social security. Otherwise they might be living on the street. In my opinion we should be striving to make social security better each year. We should be striving for early retirement. This early retirement would shrink the work force. And lead to full employment. Instead we get these Mickey Mouse proposals that end up hurting our economy and do nothing to solve our problems.

What are the powers to be in Washington thinking about? I also do not trust all the detractors of social security and simply say nuts to them. I would be interested in seeing two things from these detractors: 1) their military record and 2) their income. I believe most of these detractors have not served in the military and their income will surpass 106,800 dollars. I believe, their opinions are not formulated in doing good work for the governed. Increasing their own wealth is their prime motivator. I believe, we are in a war. As with all wars there are winners and losers. Then and only then the peace negotiators arrive. But, first one side cries uncle. Right now we, the American citizens, are the side that is losing. If we don't fight back think of the consequences. Unemployment will remain high. Our social security will be in peril and our government will start cutting social security pay and benefits. The rich will continue to pay a very small percentage of their income to social security. While the poor and middle class will continue to pay a much higher percentage of their wages to support social security. How is that fair? We will have to listen to our leaders tell us what a bad and failed idea social security is. We the American citizens will become more and more depressed and feel like disenfranchised citizens. In wars their are leaders. In this war we must start as a ground swell. This is a hard concept for the average American citizen to understand. It must happen if we are to win back America. From the groundswell I truly expect leaders to emerge (but only after enough voting support is gathered). If the politicians cry uncle (voted out of office) we win. Then we can take America back.

Our problems are unique to the age we live in. Our forefathers did not have the technology we have today. They also did not have all the lobbyist we have today. I believe, most of their decisions were based on what they thought was best for America. We have developed this political system that allows paid lobbyist to greatly influence, if not write, the bills that are passed in Congress. I believe, today's politicians for the most part try to keep us in the dark. Many of their proposals are not based on what is best for the average American citizen (if they were I would not write this book and you would not read it). Many of our public servants are held to a very high standard. Policemen, firemen, teachers and nurses to name a few are all working for the good of the

American people. They also have to develop plans that do not involve lobbyist (I know there are unions). As a nurse I know that our care plans do not involve gaining benefits thru lobbyist. Our care plans are based on what is best for the patients. And I believe those other disciplines are also dedicated and work for the common good of society.

So why are our governing bodies standards lower? There are so many workable solutions to our problems that don't increase our national debt. Common sense should tell us that pumping money into the economy will not eliminate any of our problems. But instead will cause more problems. Hell if they want to dump money into the economy then give every citizen who makes less than 106,800 dollars 50,000 dollars. It would probably be less expensive than their current plans and these people would spend the money. In my opinion, the trickle down theory does not work and never has. The corporations pocket most of the money and our national debt soars out of control. Or if giving $50,000 to our citizens who make less than $106,800 was too expensive you could dump the money in social security and offer earlier full retirement, raises for current retirees and so on.

Let's review our changes we have made in this book. When I started this book I stated I would offer doable solutions to our most pressing problems: 1) unemployment 2) health care for all Americans 3) our national debt 4) dependence on foreign oil 5) our environment 6) early full retirement 7) our social security system 8) an equitable way to pay for all these problems 9) one parent families 10) employers and employees not working together as a team 11) workers retiring at an older and older age 12) a growing population of poor Americans 13) a worse lifestyle for many Americans 14) our apathy and 15) our politicians not doing their jobs. I think I have offered you doable solutions to all those problems. You can agree or disagree. But, you must admit I did what I said I would at the beginning of the book.

We have introduced 3% worth of sales tax. But, since there would be no health care premiums most Americans would pay the 3% and still have more money. Our economy would be stimulated. Our seniors would be retiring earlier and earlier. Our health care would be better. Our society would be a better place to live and raise a family. I believe, our politicians will hate me, our corporations, their lobbyist and most wealthy Americans will also hate me for writing this book. If we are able to change the status quo in Washington we the citizens will have a real voice in our government. And most citizens would be much better off. And the country would be much better off.

Looking back in my book I realized I have chastised modern day politicians. Suppose I am wrong. In other words. Let me take a few minutes to play the devil's advocate. Suppose I am completely wrong about our leaders in Washington. Let's also assume that the politicians just didn't think of my solutions. And once they were informed of these solutions they acted on them. They use my approach to make social security fair and equitable and solvent. They re-work our health care bill and start paying our national debt using a national sales tax. Early and full retirement is begun. They re-work welfare where having one parent baby factories is no longer profitable. And two parent families become the norm. Suppose most of today's politicians sincerely want to serve their country and their citizens. Suppose they do all the things in this book. If this would happen then I apologize to all our representatives. I don't believe there is much of a chance for any of that to happen when we first notify our representatives. And we inform them of our solutions. I have been wrong more than once in my life. If that were to happen than we would solve our problems without having to have a revolution. And I say that would be great. In all honesty I don't think this will happen.

In an attempt to be fair I thought I needed to include this possibility. I am a little puzzled that these solutions have not been bought up or talked about. My background is currently in nursing. I also have a teaching certificate. Both these professions demand practical solutions within a certain time frame. For example, nurses model is known as a care plan. Every two weeks my patients have an updated care plan. Our care plans start with addressing the patient and their problems. We then pick a specific problem and we plan on how to solve this problem within a certain time frame. The problem and solution must be measurable. We then implement our solution. We set a goal. And then we evaluate to see if the solution was effective or not and to see if our goal was met. Is the problem resolved, ongoing, or does it need to be re-evaluated with a new solution. In teaching we did much of the same type thing only we called our plan a lesson plan. Both, nursing and teaching deal with problems. Nurses assess the problems, then diagnosis the problem, then plan on how to solve the problem, then implement our plan, and then we evaluate to see if our plan worked (this needs to be done within a specific time frame with measurable goals).

For example, in assessing a patient we find a pressure sore on their coccyx, the sore is superficial and we have seen many of these types of pressure ulcers. We feel the reasons for this ulcers is pressure, our patient has become incontinent and his appetite has become poor. Our diagnosis becomes decubitus ulcer on coccyx 1.0 cm long by 0.5 cm wide and 0.2 cm deep no odor or drainage. Our planning is to reduce pressure, improve nutrition and treat his wound. Our implementation begins when we call the physician. And request the following: cleanse wound on coccyx with wound cleaner and apply a duoderm dressing. Change this dressing every 3 days and prn for the next 14 days or until healed, we will order a low air loss mattress (this mattress relieves pressure) and a cushion for his wheel chair. We will also request a dietary order of milk shakes 3 times a day and vitamin E once daily. We will check the patient at least every 2 hours take him to the bathroom and do good peri care. We then begin treating the patient and at our next care plan update we will add this problem and discuss with our team. We then evaluate each week to see if the wound is improving, healed or is getting worse and we then need to re-evaluate. If the wound is healed the problem becomes resolved. If the wound remains it becomes an ongoing problem. If the wound is healed we then address preventive measures. If it is ongoing we may have to start the whole process over until we are able to resolve the problem. Some problems are irresolvable, but we keep trying to improve the patient's life regardless. Eventually most problems are resolved.

When we have our care plans each discipline has their own set of problems for the patient. For example, the social worker may inform of us family problems we did not know about. And the chaplain may inform us of funeral plans and so on. They write up their portion of the care plan as the nurses do. Now when we talk about the patients as a team in our team meeting every Wednesday with a doctor present we offer each other solutions and if someone has a good idea that becomes part of the patient's care plan. We start implementing our updated care plan at our next visit with the patient.

My problem with politicians is I don't see this attention to detail. I also don't see them working as a team to solve the problems that we the masses of American citizens are facing on a daily basis. I don't see them coming up with workable solutions and implementing them. What I do see is an annual address by the President. He tells us all the things he wishes to accomplish. Then the other political party tells us his ideas are not very good. And they have a better plan. And in the end neither side gets anything done. I refer to plans without action as crap. And so we now have a lot of crap and the American people suffer. In nursing we studied Maslow's theory. His theory has to with a hierarchy of human needs with the most basic needs to be filled before we go on the next need. For example, our most basic needs would be things like oxygen, water, food and so on, if this need is not met we will not go onto the next need. Our next need would be things like safety, warmth, shelter and so on. After these physiological needs are met then we advance to our higher needs. So his concept goes something like this. We resolve our physiological needs, then our safety and security needs, then loving and belonging needs, our needs for self esteem and after all that the ultimate need of self-actualization (this goal is not met by many). It is a person that is autonomous, motivated. Not self centered, able to solve problems and is able to work for the good of others. Many of our citizens do not have even the most basic needs. A poor person living on the street in a cardboard box is a good example. Many of our citizens now lack jobs and are unable to climb Maslow's hierarchy of human needs.

That is why I have been so hard on our government. They are not helping their citizens enough. Our representatives need their own care plans. They need to meet weekly, implement their plans, then evaluate every two weeks. If this were being done along with my interventions I believe we would solve most of America's problems.

I have tried not to be too negative in this book and have a sense of humor at the same time. I often watch Judge Judy on television and she is always asking "Do you know how to tell when a teenager is lying?" and her answer is "When their lips are moving". I often think that way about our politicians. I do not know if I am in alone in my thinking, but I believe many citizens feel that way as well. And when you stop to think about it that is a very sad commentary about our politicians and the political system they have created for themselves. I have tried to enumerate in this book what I think our solutions should be: 1) contact your elected officials by whatever means you can. Let him or her know of the solutions we have discussed in this book. Let him or her know you are serious. When they continue to keep us in gridlock, vote all incumbents out of office. See if they begin to feel like their job is on the line if they don't start working for the masses. I feel their jobs should be on the line if they don't break the gridlock and pass meaningful legislation. And the bills should be short and to the point (no longer than 3 pages or a girls dress and their should be no add ons). If a bill is worth voting on it should be written as a bill and passed or rejected on its on merits. When a bill has numerous sections and becomes complicated I get very suspicious. I asked myself what are we really getting in this bill? Remember the candy kiss (keep it simple stupid).

Chapter 10

I have two concerns as to whether any of my solutions will be noticed. They are pride and apathy. The pride I speak of is in every American, at least that is what I believe. I believe we are proud to be Americans. That we are proud of our parents, grandparents, children, their children and their children's children. Most of us have seen a dance recital or a little league sporting event. We went because one of the children playing or dancing was somehow related. We watched that child and if he/she did something good we were pumping our chest and cheering them on or applauding. If they made a mistake we consoled them and then encouraged them to keep trying. We did not disown them. We need to be able to be proud of our government, like when it really was our government by the people and for the people. If our government is going to work we need to be active.

I keep referring to my America. In my America the problems I have outlined in this book would be solved. And I would be more proud of my heritage than I am now. And pride is one of the things we must restore in every citizen. The sense that this is my America should belong to all of us. The idea that this is our government and it should be working for the citizens who elected it must be restored. The idea that the citizens are actually involved in dictating policies. These are all the things that need to be done if we are going to take back America and restore it to its greatest heights. If we are going to point to America and say with pride that this is my America then we have to become proactive. I am appalled at what our governing bodies are trying to do to us by their inaction which leads to acceptance on our part. This acceptance on our part is no less than apathy which at this point in time we cannot afford. So if we remain apathetic should we expect anything more from our governing bodies? If we are to enact changes we must be active and must use communication. We must follow our game plan. And then and only then will we see results. I kind of got ahead of myself and mixed in apathy with pride but, then again I am no writer.

In apathy I see the one character flaw that could doom this country. I believe, if we are to make meaningful changes then the masses must rise. They must let the politicians know they are not going to take it anymore. The corruption must end. There must be more important things than how much money can I make and how to get reelected. If we must use our 2x4's and sling shots to get these points across than so be it. To me inaction is the same as acceptance which equals apathy. I believe given a game plan most Americans are ready to act. Our courageous forefathers have fought in many wars for this country. I believe, we need take up arms (computers, cells, faxes, pen and paper, text, twitter whatever).

If we are to find our America than we need only to act. If we are to be governed as our Declaration of Independence indicates we should be, we need to take a more active roll. No longer is it good enough just to vote. I have been a voter for a long time and felt like I was doing my part. I no longer feel that way because I believe both political parties are so corrupt and uncaring that if they are not enlightened by an angry America they will only act in their best interest and the citizens can go straight to hell.

When I think because of our government policies we were forced to borrow money from China I become very upset. So upset I am going to learn how to e-mail, go on line and post something, twitter and text. To think we fought a war cut taxes and borrowed trillions of dollars to fight this war makes no sense to me. Cutting taxes while fighting a war, driving up our national debt instead of funding our own war is that not crazy? Rewarding banks for giving out risky loans is that not crazy? Investing our money in unworthy companies in a hopes of solving unemployment is that not crazy? When Solyndra went bankrupt how many millions or billions did we give them? What did we get in return from all these policies. A country on the verge of defaulting on all its loans. I only went back as far as the last 2 presidents and our representatives for these examples and there are so many more. Why is that? I believe we can easily fix our problems but with our current leaders we will not. That is why I keep repeating myself. Remember, we the citizens make up America. America is not the politicians, the courts, the system of government but America is made up by its everyday citizens. America is the melting pot made up by all of its citizens no matter race, religion, level of income and our representation is most surly lacking at this point in time. If we are to make America a better place then we need to act and act now!

Chapter 11

Here's another thought about social security and full employment. When we did our 800 billion dollar stimulus and tried our trickle down approach that clearly did not work, what would have happened if we if we had put that money into social security, given raises to our retirees and offered full retirement at age 62. I believe, we would have had many more people retiring. Our seniors would have more money to spend. Someone would have to take the retirees' jobs. There would be a whole industry opening up. With fewer workers and more consumers would this not stimulate the economy and decrease or completely eliminate unemployment. I think that is a good thing.

Now President Obama's job proposal came out. He is going to use the trickle down with tax relief for business and individuals. Pour more money into bridges and roads (where, oh where, has my gas tax on every gallon of gas gone that is supposed to keep our bridges and roads repaired). He is going to add more money for teachers, firemen and policemen (is this the federal government's job or are these state issues?). In any event if it were handled correctly I could live with helping these entities, but I do not think we would need the federal government's help if they would just use some common sense. These type of remedies do not go to the heart of the problem, and add more to our national debt. I believe these measures will help President Obama's election campaign, but in the long run are bad for America.

Where, oh where is Abraham Lincoln, a president that was hated by many during his presidency, but made hard decisions based on what he thought was best for America. I believe, the jobs President Obama is advocating are just the type of phony temporary jobs that cause more harm than good. They are an easy sell in my opinion. I also don't believe we need a 59 page rebuttal by the republicans who also have no permanent fixes. I don't hear any of them saying lets pay our fair share of social security. I don't hear any of them saying if we had less workers and more consumers we would reduce unemployment and stimulate the economy all without the use of federal money. I believe the reason why we don't hear this is it would cost our politicians money and hurt their election campaigns.

If our government feels a need to pour more money into our jobs programs then let them put that 700 billion dollars into social security and offer any worker 62 and over full retirement with full benefits if they quit working within 1 year from when they start drawing their benefits. This would give the retiree enough time to build a nest egg. They would retire young enough to become great consumers. Employers would now have a huge portion of the workforce retiring each year and would need to hire employees. We would have real permanent jobs on a yearly basis that needed to be filled. Lets start looking at the forest and not the trees. When thinking about our problems in a nursing vein I keep thinking the politicians are looking at huge open wounds and they are trying to fix these wounds by covering them with band aides. When the band aides fall off they replace them with more band aides. If you are going to treat these wounds (social security, unemployment and so on you know all the ones we talked about) you have to clean the wounds (get rid of the incumbents). Then pack the wounds (elect new representatives). Then treat and inspect the wounds weekly to see if the wounds are healing (check on the newly elected). Then re-evaluate the process (let the newly elected know how they are doing). Once healed we use protective or preventive treatments (continue to stay in touch with the newly elected). Then and only then can real healing take place.

A couple of more comments on President Obama's job speech. He wants a proposal to be passed. He started without a bill when he came on television. He did not yet have a bill. How are we going to pass and pay for a proposal? Are we going to float more treasury notes and have China buy them? The second comment seems so obvious I don't feel I should have to make it but I will anyway. So here goes. Businesses do not hire employees because of tax breaks. Let me say that again businesses do not hire employees because of tax breaks. Businesses hire employees when their business expands and when there is an increase in demand for their product that they cannot meet with their current staff of employees. In other words, they hire people when they need more staff to get the work done. Let's take that a step further. If the economy is not expanding and if they are not increasing their business they will not hire more employees. Under those circumstances tax breaks are useless as far as unemployment goes.

Now under this nonexpanding, no more demand economy when the employer receives these tax breaks he thanks the politicians, owes them a favor and pockets the money. How does that increase jobs? I do not believe it increases jobs one bit. I believe this is one of the misconceptions we have been fed for so many years that if you close your eyes you might start believing it too. Quit spending money we don't have on things we don't need (that approach should be limited to my wife). I expect more from our President (I voted for him). I believe using this approach, corporations and manufactures would pocket more money and our national debt would rise. I believe, the overall effect on unemployment would be very minimal. I believe, the overall effect would be more wealth for the wealthy and more debt for our country. Are we selling America to China?

I wrote about the job proposal as soon as I saw it. As it turns out, President Obama wants to finance these jobs by taxes. He is going to try to tax the wealthiest Americans using some sort of income tax (good luck on that). I see the republicans fighting him on this, much name calling, and nothing coming from this. I have had only two semesters of college economics and that was well over twenty years ago so I don't feel like an expert. The one thing I can remember (at least partially) is the law of supply and demand. I have not looked this up but I think it goes something like this: If you have more demand than supply—supplies will increase until the demand is equal to the supplies. Things that might happened when the demand is higher than the supply are: 1) prices may go up 2) more workers might be added to the workforce 3) wages and benefits might increase to get enough workers. When supply is greater than demand things that might happen are: 1) prices might go down 2) layoffs might occur 3) benefits and wages might go down. We quit adding more supply until supply equals demand.

As I see it the problem is to keep the demand high. When you have earlier and earlier retirement coupled with the unemployed taking these retiree permanent jobs you, in essence, have increased the number of consumers and reduced the workforce. Those two items alone will increase the demand for goods and services. I feel increased demand for consumer goods coupled with a smaller available workforce is a very good thing for all Americans. If this is so, why are we increasing retirement age? If you say cost, think about the 800 billion dollars we used to stimulate the economy last year. Think about 450 billion we want to use this year. These stimulus are for temporary jobs that in my opinion do more harm than good and have no lasting effect. Think about reworking social security as I described. I keep thinking we are backwards in our economic plans. Then again I am not an economist. I don't think any of their plans have worked so maybe someone else needs to show them the way. And my thinking is related to the candy kiss (keep it simple stupid). I believe my thinking is correct. I listen to all these complicated plans and wonder who is getting a kick back? Why are the plans so long and the language that sounds foreign to me (what are they covering up). I may not be the brightest candle burning but I have been around the block a time or two, so don't give me baloney and call it steak. I am not so old and feeble that I cannot tell the difference. I believe that most, if not all, the employment, social security and other fixes coming out of Washington are pure baloney, dressed in fancy packages, but baloney none the less.

Many of our economic experts offer ideas for job creation that include making it easier to borrow money, reducing regulations for construction, increasing tax credits and reducing environmental regulations. I believe none of these solutions really address our unemployment problems. Making it too easy to borrow money was a component in our banking collapse. So is that really a great idea? Many of our regulations on construction for environmental reasons, safety reasons and so on are very much needed. Removing those regulations is a bad idea. Tax credits do not create jobs. I believe, none of these ideas actually creates jobs. As I stated before, what I believe creates jobs is found simply in the law of supply and demand. Tax breaks are great for the corporations and our representatives. The corporations can put the money from the tax break in their pocket. Our representatives now have corporations that owe them a favor. None of that creates jobs. If you have a product and there is a huge demand for this product that is not being met you will find a way to meet that demand. If that way of meeting that demand includes hiring additional workers you will. I believe that is what drives job creation. Sounds simple doesn't it?

I read about all the unemployed and it breaks my heart. The stories are so sad. Yet, when I check our census against our unemployment projections I find a direct correlation. I have included some charts for you, the American public, to compare and come to your own conclusions. My conclusions are simple if we encouraged full early retirement and reduced the retirement age at which we could do this to 62 we would be able to shrink the workforce. This would create less unemployment. Our newly retired seniors would become great consumers. Our newly employed population would become great consumers. Those two thing alone would increase demand on consumer goods. I believe this increased demand would increase jobs in order to keep up with the demand.

When I compared some of these charts I came up with some interesting tidbits. I was able to find the completed 2000 census. I looked by age groupings. In age 50-54 that was 6.2% of our population. In age grouping 55-59 that was 4.8% of our population. If you ad the 2 groupings together 6.2 and 4.8 I believe that comes to 11%.

It is now 11 years later so the 50-54 year group would be for the most part in the 60-64 grouping and 55-59 year olds would be in 65-69. If both these groups were all retired where would unemployment be? If this entire group were retired we would have more consumers and less workers. Would this not wipe out unemployment? Would this not create more demand than supply on many consumer goods? As our population increases we need to decrease retirement age. Our population has been growing the last 3 census and we have been increasing retirement age is that not a formula for double digit unemployment? Is that not just the opposite of what we should be doing? I believe, with the 1% national sales tax for social security we would be adding at least several billion dollars a year to social security. That, plus everyone paying their fair share by lifting the $106,800 cap where you stop paying and adding a cap of no one receiving more than $100,000 a year, would all make early full retirement very real. The early full retirement would shrink the workforce and would increase the demand for consumer goods.

Of all the problems I have written about in this book I believe, the unemployment problem to be the most important at this time. I also believe the unemployment problem to be the easiest to fix. The way I want to fix the unemployment is with real permanent jobs (not phony temporary costly jobs). I believe, the reasons I am able to come up these solutions to our unemployment problem and our politicians have not are: 1) I am looking at our unemployment problem as a care plan and I am looking for real permanent solutions. I do not have to worry about my election campaign. 2) I do not care whose toes I step on. 3) my solutions will not cost me money (except for the sales tax). 4) I have no lobbyist to answer to and 5) I played the what if we did this game over and over until things started to click. I believe, our representatives do not look at our problems as care plans because their real interests are only how does this make me more money or help my election campaign. If these items are not addressed in processing a bill these politicians are not interested. I believe if the masses do not bring solutions forward they will not be brought forward. I believe, The solutions that will be shoved down our throat are the ones that help lobbyist, make politicians more money and help the wealthy. Think about this. How is it fair that the rich make the laws that we must live with? When our forefathers were forced into service many did the right thing only because it was the right thing to do. When was the last time a president did that?

I have added my five bills that I have written to the back of the book. So you can look at them again. Perhaps cut them out send them to your representatives with as many signatures as you can get. Or make fun of them. Its your choice.

QT-P1. **Age Groups and Sex: 2000**
Data Set: Census 2000 Summary File 1 (SF 1) 100-Percent Data
Geographic Area: **United States**

Age	Number			Percent			Males per 100 females
	Both sexes	Male	Female	Both sexes	Male	Female	
Total population	**281,421,906**	**138,053,563**	**143,368,343**	**100.0**	**100.0**	**100.0**	**96.3**
Under 5 years	19,175,798	9,810,733	9,365,065	6.8	7.1	6.5	104.8
5 to 9 years	20,549,505	10,523,277	10,026,228	7.3	7.6	7.0	105.0
10 to 14 years	20,528,072	10,520,197	10,007,875	7.3	7.6	7.0	105.1
15 to 19 years	20,219,890	10,391,004	9,828,886	7.2	7.5	6.9	105.7
20 to 24 years	18,964,001	9,687,814	9,276,187	6.7	7.0	6.5	104.4
25 to 29 years	19,381,336	9,798,760	9,582,576	6.9	7.1	6.7	102.3
30 to 34 years	20,510,388	10,321,769	10,188,619	7.3	7.5	7.1	101.3
35 to 39 years	22,706,664	11,318,696	11,387,968	8.1	8.2	7.9	99.4
40 to 44 years	22,441,863	11,129,102	11,312,761	8.0	8.1	7.9	98.4
45 to 49 years	20,092,404	9,889,506	10,202,898	7.1	7.2	7.1	96.9
50 to 54 years	17,585,548	8,607,724	8,977,824	6.2	6.2	6.3	95.9
55 to 59 years	13,469,237	6,508,729	6,960,508	4.8	4.7	4.9	93.5
60 to 64 years	10,805,447	5,136,627	5,668,820	3.8	3.7	4.0	90.6
65 to 69 years	9,533,545	4,400,362	5,133,183	3.4	3.2	3.6	85.7
70 to 74 years	8,857,441	3,902,912	4,954,529	3.1	2.8	3.5	78.8
75 to 79 years	7,415,813	3,044,456	4,371,357	2.6	2.2	3.0	69.6
80 to 84 years	4,945,367	1,834,897	3,110,470	1.8	1.3	2.2	59.0
85 to 89 years	2,789,818	876,501	1,913,317	1.0	0.6	1.3	45.8
90 years and over	1,449,769	350,497	1,099,272	0.5	0.3	0.8	31.9
Under 18 years	72,293,812	37,059,196	35,234,616	25.7	26.8	24.6	105.2
18 to 64 years	174,136,341	86,584,742	87,551,599	61.9	62.7	61.1	98.9
18 to 24 years	27,143,454	13,873,829	13,269,625	9.6	10.0	9.3	104.6
25 to 44 years	85,040,251	42,568,327	42,471,924	30.2	30.8	29.6	100.2
25 to 34 years	39,891,724	20,120,529	19,771,195	14.2	14.6	13.8	101.8
35 to 44 years	45,148,527	22,447,798	22,700,729	16.0	16.3	15.8	98.9
45 to 64 years	61,952,636	30,142,586	31,810,050	22.0	21.8	22.2	94.8
45 to 54 years	37,677,952	18,497,230	19,180,722	13.4	13.4	13.4	96.4
55 to 64 years	24,274,684	11,645,356	12,629,328	8.6	8.4	8.8	92.2
65 years and over	34,991,753	14,409,625	20,582,128	12.4	10.4	14.4	70.0
65 to 74 years	18,390,986	8,303,274	10,087,712	6.5	6.0	7.0	82.3
75 to 84 years	12,361,180	4,879,353	7,481,827	4.4	3.5	5.2	65.2
85 years and over	4,239,587	1,226,998	3,012,589	1.5	0.9	2.1	40.7
16 years and over	217,149,127	105,134,229	112,014,898	77.2	76.2	78.1	93.9
18 years and over	209,128,094	100,994,367	108,133,727	74.3	73.2	75.4	93.4
21 years and over	196,899,193	94,737,132	102,162,061	70.0	68.6	71.3	92.7
60 years and over	45,797,200	19,546,252	26,250,948	16.3	14.2	18.3	74.5
62 years and over	41,256,029	17,373,013	23,883,016	14.7	12.6	16.7	72.7
67 years and over	31,101,522	12,594,818	18,506,704	11.1	9.1	12.9	68.1
75 years and over	16,600,767	6,106,351	10,494,416	5.9	4.4	7.3	58.2
Median age (years)	35.3	34.0	36.5	(X)	(X)	(X)	(X)

(X) Not applicable.
Source: U.S. Census Bureau, Census 2000 Summary File 1, Matrices P13 and PCT12.

U.S. Population by Sex and Age
Profile of General Demographic Characteristics, Census 2000 and Census 2010

Sex and age	Number, 2000	Percent	Number, 2010	Percent
Total population	**281,421,906**	**100.0%**	**308,745,538**	**100.0%**
Male	138,053,563	49.1	151,781,326	49.2
Female	143,368,343	50.9	156,964,212	50.8
Under 5 years	19,175,798	6.8	20,201,362	6.5
5 to 9 years	20,549,505	7.3	20,348,657	6.6
10 to 14 years	20,528,072	7.3	20,677,194	6.7
15 to 19 years	20,219,890	7.2	22,040,343	7.1
20 to 24 years	18,964,001	6.7	21,585,999	7.0
25 to 34 years	39,891,724	14.2	41,063,948	13.3
35 to 44 years	45,148,527	16.0	41,070,606	13.3
45 to 54 years	37,677,952	13.4	45,006,716	14.6
55 to 59 years	13,469,237	4.8	19,664,805	6.4
60 to 64 years	10,805,447	3.8	16,817,924	5.4
65 to 74 years	18,390,986	6.5	21,713,429	7.0
75 to 84 years	12,361,180	4.4	13,061,122	4.2
85 years and over	4,239,587	1.5	5,493,433	1.8
Median age (years)	35.3	n.a.	37.2	n.a.
18 years and over	209,128,094	74.3	234,564,071	76.0
21 years and over	196,899,193	70.0	220,958,853	71.6
62 years and over	41,256,029	14.7	49,972,181	16.2
65 years and over	34,991,753	12.4	40,267,984	13.0

NOTES: (—) represents zero or rounds to zero; n.a. = not applicable.
Source: U.S. Census Bureau, Census 2000 and Census 2010. Web: www.census.gov .

Read more: U.S. Population by Sex and Age, Census 2000 — Infoplease.com
http://www.infoplease.com/ipa/A0884102.html#ixzz1b4V1yc2a

Here is a sample of my health care bill:

Health care bill number 3215
Section I
Who is covered
The mechanics of the bill / how is it paid for
What is covered
Section II
Who is in charge of the bill
Section III
Exceptions and limitations
Section IV
Hospice/Medicare/Medicaid
Section VI
Review

Section I

1) All Americans citizens at the time of birth are covered. So there are no preexisting conditions to consider. All Americans receive a health care card that can be swiped like a credit card. All approved health care providers will be linked to these health care cards. All Americans will receive a health care card and a handbook at time of birth and all American citizens will be issued the health care cards and handbooks when this health care bill goes into effect. The health care handbook would explain what is covered and where to go for treatment. All medical conditions are covered with the patient or patient's family deciding how aggressive the treatment should be. Education

with the doctor and medical team would be an available option for all Americans.

2) The bill is paid for by a 1% sales tax on every item sold in the United States (including online purchases). This revenue would be put into treasury bonds and put into a special health care account. The money in this account can only be used for health care services and will not be put into any general revenue account. Any use of this money other than medical claims will be considered an act of treason and prosecuted as such.

Section II

1) A medical advisory board will be formed and charred by the whip and majority leaders in Washington. They will have equal authority. They will be responsible for investigating claims. All claims will be linked to the internet and only approved health care providers will have this link. The committee will designate state investigators for on sight inspection on any questionable claims.

Section III

1) Limitations and exceptions—Limitations illegal immigrants are not eligible. Exceptions—True medical emergencies, as defined in the health care hand book will be treated for all including illegal immigrants.

Section IV

1) Hospice, Medicare, and Medicaid will not change.

Section V

1) The medical committee will meet every month and review claims, and revenue versus expenditures and make recommendations how to best implement our delivery system.

Here is a sample of our national Dept Reduction bill 33

Section I purpose
Section II how is the bill financed
Section III who has access to the funds and their distribution

Section I

1) The bill is for the express purpose of paying down our national debt

Section II

1) the bill will be financed by a 1% national sales tax on every item sold in the United States (including online purchases)

Section III

1) The United States treasurer and his/her representative will have access the funds in this sales tax fund that has been created to assist in paying the United States national debt down.

2) The funds from this account will be collected no later than the 5th of the following month and used in the repayment of our National Debt (all other use or uses of this account is strictly prohibited with mandatory prison sentences of 25 years to life for anyone who violates this use).

Social security adjustment bill 3711 is as follows:

I Lifting the income ceiling on social security
II Applying a cap on social security money that can be paid out in a one year period.
III A sales tax for social security.
IV Who will administer this bill

Section I

1) The 106,800 dollar income cap, where you stop paying social security will be removed with no ceiling cap in it's place. For example if you earn 17 million dollars a year you will pay social security on 17 million dollars a year as will your employer. And the percentage you pay on social security will remain the same no matter the dollar amount you earn. The money generated from removing this cap will be put into purchasing treasury bonds and put into a special social security account.

Section II

1) There will be a cap of 100,000 dollars that can be paid out to any one retiree in a one year period.

Section III

1) There will be a 1% national sales tax on all items purchased in the United States (including on line purchases). The money from this sales tax will go into purchasing treasury bonds. And added to a special social security account. This will be the same account that all social security revenue is in. The social security account will not be placed in or used for anything other than funds for retirement. The revenue from this social security account is forbidden from being placed into general revenue and used for anything than it's intended purposes. The intended purposes for the money in the social security account are: 1) Lower full early retirement age 2) Give raises to retirees.

Section IV

The social security administration will be responsible for oversight of this revenue. They will analysis census figures, plus all the new revenue and calculate at what age they can offer full early retirement, raises to retirees and keep social security solvent. Any other use of the revenue will be strictly forbidden and punished by a mandatory 25 to life prison term for any offender.

Reducing dependence on foreign oil and cleaning our environment bill number 5907

- I   Forming a clean air board with duties and obligations
- II   Limitations, qualifications and salaries
- III 0% emissions bill
- IV provisions for charging stations

Section I

1) Each state will have a clean air board. The board will be made up of 5 members. Each member will have an equal vote. And they will pick their own chairman or chairwoman. Their duties will include testing our air quality daily. They will have the power to impose fines, suspend, and terminate licenses for repeat offenders. They also be able to make recommendations and purpose legislation for the citizens to vote on. The board members will meet at least monthly to go over their findings, recommendations and new business. There will be a mandated 0% emission law in place that they will be in charge of enforcing.

Section II

Limitations

No one with ties to manufactures, oil companies, and/or utilities will be allowed to serve on this board. No paid lobbyist will be allowed to contact members of this board. Paid lobbyist will not be allowed to submit proposals or request.

The board members will be paid a salary that is agreed on by the governor of each state not to exceed $75,000 a year. The board members will take a civil servants test before being hired. Veterans will be given a 50 point bonus. The 5 highest scores will be offered these jobs and if someone refuses when offered the next highest scoring person will be offered the job until all the positions are filled.

Section III

0% emission bill

All car manufacturers that sell cars in the United States will have to sell at least 10% of their fleet that produce 0% emissions by 2013. Each ensuing year until 2018 an additional 10% of their fleet must produce 0% emissions. So by 2014, 20% of our cars being manufactured and sold would have 0% emissions, by 2015, 30% of our cars manufactured and sold would have 0% emissions, by 2016, 40% of our cars manufactured and sold would have 0% emissions, and by 2017, 50% of our cars manufactured and sold in the United States would have 0% emissions. Once our cars that had 0% emissions reached 50% in the United States we would be allowed to increase that percentage but never decrease that percentage.

Section IV

Electric charging stations would be able to charge the customers 30% more than what they were paying to the utilities that would service these stations. Charging stations would be allowed at all gas stations.

Here is a sample of my Aide to Dependent Children Amendment: ADC Aide to Dependent Children Amendment

I Who is eligible:

1) One parent families and two parent families
2) How the benefits now differ for one parent families and two parent families

One parent families that earn less than what considered the current poverty level will be eligible for $3,500 assistance from social security annually for the first 5 years of their first child's life. Any children beyond the first born to a one parent family will not eligible for any additional benefits.

Two parent families that stay together and raise their children and earn less than the current poverty level will be eligible for $3,500 annually from social security for the first 10 years of their first two children's life. ($7,000 a year maximum). No additional money will be rewarded for more than 2 children. If during this period the two parent families rises above the poverty level the government will continue these subsidies. For the entire 10 years. All families are eligible for free contraceptives and sex education as provided by our national health care.

Chapter 12

I believe the reasons I or someone else could write short, clear bills that the average American citizen can understand is because I owe no allegiance to any lobbyist or other group. I believe the reason that the politicians make their bills so long and confusing is they have to be careful not to hurt any lobbyist that supports them and any of their other supporters. They are also able to add onto bills items that would help their friends and lobbyist. This also lengthens and makes bills more confusing. Since I don't care about lobbyist or any other groups and my only motive is to do the right thing, my bills are short and to the point. I would like to see some of our current politicians get motivated enough to pass legislation that is short, clear, nothing added on because it is the right thing to do. I would like to see some of our politicians doing the right thing for our citizens for no other reason than it is the right thing to do. Should we expect less from our representatives?

I read 100 pages of president Obama's health care bill and I only have an inkling of what it said. The bill, as far as I can tell, keeps private health care insurance companies. But since the bill is 1,018 pages of the longest mumble jumble I have ever read I cannot decipher it. I believe, the bill talks about opting out, in network, out of network, preexisting conditions and overall is so complicated that the average American citizen has no idea what the bill is saying. My question is why does the bill have to be so complicated? Please look at the bills I have written.

I read countless descriptions of President Obama's jobs bill. I thought about printing all the bills that corresponds to my bills and placing them side by side. But the book would have been way too long, the health care bill alone is over a 1,000 pages. I could not have afforded to have the book published.

I truly believe if we incorporated into law the five bills I have written we would solve most of Americas problems.

I began writing this book before President Obama came up with his job proposal. I was so shocked when he came out with the figures he did for the job proposal. He is requesting 450 billion dollars (roughly). He then ask if anyone is opposed to this bill and why? I am very much opposed to this job proposal because of its ineffectual use of the money being proposed. If he is able to get 450 billion dollars, why would we create temporary jobs? Once I took a look at the amount of money he is proposing and compared it to our population I had a couple of other ideas come to my mind: 1) there are approximately 65 million people in the United States who are 55 years of age or older. Of that number approximately 25 million are less than 65 years old and the other 40 million are 65 or older. I realize that some citizens work longer than 65 and some retire early so as a rough estimate lets assume that all the citizens 65 and older are retired and all the rest are still working. That would mean we would have 25 million Americans 55 and older still working. What would happen if these 25 million Americans would retire immediately? Would that not open up 25 million real jobs? If we dumped 450 billion of dollars into social security and followed my social security bill I believe, we could give all retirees raises and offer full social security benefits for all citizens 55 and over. I also believe we could pay these retirees a decent retirement amount with all the additional revenue we would now have. 2) With the amount of money our last two Presidents have squandered, please, lets not waste this money and

5 years down the road wonder where the money went. Just for fun lets look at some of the money these Presidents have spent. Bush's stimulus packages included: 300 billion to American home owners, 178 billion to American tax payers, 29 billion to bail out Bear Sterns, 200 billion to Fannie May and Freddie Mac, 150 billion to AIG, and 700 billion to bail out banks. Mr. Bush also fought a war while giving these tax breaks and he borrowed money to fight this war. When I read about the amount he borrowed for this war it is somewhere between 750 million and 3 trillion depending on your source. I have read both and I believe neither. So why is it that Mr. Bush would deem a war necessary and then not have the courage to have Congress fund this war? In the short term borrowing money for financing a war and giving tax breaks looks great. But in the long term our National debt soars and the tax breaks have little effect on our economy.

Also Mr. Bush joined in the legal battle that lead to killing the electric car. Mr. Obama is no better in my opinion. He has supported an economic stimulus of 787 billion in 2009 and this year a 450 billion jobs package. And the health care bill he is pushing is too vague, too complicated and too expensive. Both the last 2 presidents rewarded banks who were incompetently run. These banks were bailed out. Banks that were responsible did not receive a stimulus or any other reward. It seems to me that if the federal government insured the banks that failed then the government should cover the bank's investors and force these banks to file bankruptcy. The competently run banks would be rewarded with more customers and America would have less debt. It just makes sense.

Some of the proposals that are now coming out of Washington imply that if we are less diligent on protecting our environment that this will somehow increase jobs. I believe relaxing environmental restrictions to help with economic growth is a dangerous practice, would help the offending company, but would not necessarily increase demand for the product or increase jobs.

I admit I voted once for Bush and once for Obama but I do not know if the opposing candidates would have been any better. I tried to figure out how early we could offer full retirement using my formula and the money Obama is now wasting (it is too late to get the money Bush spent or Obama's first stimulus). I could not figure out the early retirement and bonuses we could offer all our citizens to retire on their birthday. My calculator does not have enough zeroes. This is strictly a guess but I think we could offer full retirement at age 55 and give each citizen a $10,000 bonus when they reach age 55 and give each retired person a $10,000 bonus. I think my estimate may be low but it will take someone more accomplished in math than me to figure that out.

In any event when the amount of money changes hands that has taken place in our last two administrations. I become very suspicious and I wonder where all this money went? Does no one see the economic mess we are in? What will our health care cost? How long will these temporary jobs last? Where is this money going? Just exactly how is 240 billion dollars in tax breaks going to create jobs? Why don't we invest in Solyndra (ops they went belly-up)? We know early retirement will increase the availability of permanent jobs. So why don't we go for a sure thing with this economic stimulus money? Besides all else the government should have a very limited scope in job creation.

What if everyone that read this book had friends and neighbors read this book and then they all signed it and sent their signed book to president Obama I wonder what would happen? Just a thought I had while on a plane. Probably the e-mails, facebooking, twitter, faxing, writing, and so on would be better. So why not do it all? I think all Americans should be involved especially the snow birds. Our country was formed on principles that included freedom from political oppression, freedom of religion and hard work. I believe we are currently being oppressed by this bred of politicians that are ruining our country. And if we do not get our sling shots and 2x4's ready we will not be able to rescue America.

I truly believe what I have written in this book is a true and accurate account of my thoughts and beliefs. Could I have made mistakes? Of course. Have I offended some? Most definitely. Do I apologize? No, I believe I have the right of freedom of speech under the first Amendment. I believe I have a right to express my beliefs, thoughts and ideas. If I have made mistakes in this book they were unintentional. The only apology is to my readers. I realize I am not a writer so my thoughts became scattered at times. I have read and reread my book many times since I wrote it. And I believe it represents a fair and accurate depiction of our current problems in America. I also believe in the solutions I wrote about.

Listen up to my final story all you David's and Danielle's. The birds are singing. The children are playing and John is approaching full retirement. He graduated 30 years ago from college and started working as an engineer jobs were easy to find he was 24. Retirement age at that time was 60. Since that time social security has had huge surpluses and Congress has gotten full retirement age down to 55. John is looking forward to his retirement as is his wife and children. John vows to stay active in keeping in contact with his political representatives. He wants his children to be able to retire at age 50. Since average life expectancy is now 90 as a direct result of our wonderful health care that all citizens enjoy John looks forward to 35 years of an active retirement (after having worked 30 years). If all goes as expected John's children will work 25 years, retire at age 50 and have 40 years of retirement. This could not happen, right. This book is not meant to be a fairy tale. It is my views of fixing America and what America could and should be.

I wrote this book using my mind and my heart. And I do not know what to expect will happen when it is published. Will everyone laugh at me? Maybe. Will anyone think I have made sense? Maybe. I know what I would like to happen and that is for this book to find an AMERICA that will read it and then take up the actions I have outlined. In any event to the people who have taken their time to read this book I thank you from the bottom of my heart. And I promise you that you will not have to undergo this torture again. This is my one and only book. To my wife who proofread the book corrected the spelling and made sentences out of some of my statements thank you. To all the David's out there thank you and remember to get your sling shots and 2x4's ready (text, twitter, cells, faxes, pen and paper, whatever means at your disposal). I was able to write a 100 pages. It was very, very hard for me a man of a few words to write as many pages as I did. If nothing else the book was as long as a girls dress (long enough to cover the subject but short enough to be interesting). Whew I am glad I got all that off my chest.